FINAL SIGNS

ED HINDSON

HARVEST HOUSE PUBLISHERS
Eugene, Oregon 97402

FINAL SIGNS

Copyright © 1996 by Harvest House Publishers
Eugene, Oregon 97402

Library of Congress Cataloging-in-Publication Data

Hindson, Edward E.
    Final signs / Ed Hindson
        p.   cm.
    Includes bibliographical references
    ISBN 1-56507-378-9 (alk. paper)
        1. Bible—Prophecies—Eschatology.   2. Second Advent.   I. Title
    BS849.E63H56   1996
    236'.9—dc20   95-44184
                                                                        CIP

Printed in the United States of America.
96 97 98 99 00 01 /BF/ 10 9 8 7 6 5 4 3 2

To

Dr. Tim LaHaye

for his personal encouragement

and his commitment to

the study of Bible prophecy

Contents

A Glimpse of Things to Come

We are living in the most incredible times the world has ever known. Live reports via satellite beam the latest events from around the globe into our living rooms every day. This technology has allowed us, for the first time in human history, to actually watch developments of great significance as they unfold. Everything from political crises to international conflicts come to us live as they are happening around the world.

Who could have imagined a few years ago that we would be able to sit in our homes and watch international conflicts take place right in front of us at the moment that they happen? We are instantly transported from Washington, D.C. to London to Moscow to Jerusalem to Baghdad in a matter of seconds. And this is probably a microcosm of things to come.

The stage is now set for the *final signs* of the end times. Changes and developments are happening so fast that we are speeding headlong toward the greatest crisis the world has ever known. Every new turn of events reminds us that "the Big One" could be just around the corner. But one of the dangers of such expectation is that it can easily lead to wild speculation that is premature and even misleading.

The purpose of this book is to examine the biblical prophecies of the end times. But it is also to raise a word of caution regarding the excessive speculations of well-meaning but non-biblical attempts to predict the future. It is my sincere desire that, no matter what perspective you have of the last days, you will benefit from this study and the accompanying words of caution. I trust as well that the information in this book and the spirit in which it is written will increase your interest in the serious study of biblical prophecy.

Along the highway, signs are used to identify locations, provide information, and give warnings. The same is true of prophetic signs. They stand out on the biblical horizon to get our attention. They give us a glimpse of things to come—but only a glimpse. Signs are not intended to give all the details of future events, yet they do play a prominent role in biblical prophecy.

As we consider these prophetic signs, it's important to recognize a key distinction. On the one hand, Scripture tells us that our Lord will come like "a thief in the night" (1 Thessalonians 5:2). His coming will occur suddenly, instantly, in the "twinkling of an eye" (1 Corinthians 15:52). It will happen so fast there will be no warning signs preceding His coming. The world will be caught by surprise when our Lord comes for His bride. The church will be raptured to glory, and unbelievers will be left behind.

On the other hand, the Bible warns us: "There will be signs in the sun, moon and stars. On the earth, nations will be in anguish and perplexity at the roaring and tossing of the sea. Men will faint from terror, apprehensive of what is coming on the world, for the heavenly bodies will be shaken. At that time they will see the Son of Man coming in a cloud with power and great glory" (Luke 21:25-27).

These warning signs clearly have to do with Christ's return in judgment on an unbelieving world. They will occur toward the end of the Great Tribulation. Therefore, as we examine these "final signs" we must remind ourselves that most of them will take place *after* the rapture of the church. This book, then, focuses on those signs that precede the final aspect of our Lord's return.

As we begin to see the potential of these final signs taking shape, we can safely assume that our Lord's coming for His church is drawing near. Jesus said, "When these things begin to take place, stand up and lift up your heads, because your redemption is drawing near" (Luke 21:28).

Keep looking up!

—Ed Hindson
There's Hope!
Atlanta, GA

Chapter 1

UNDERSTANDING
THE END TIMES

Many people believe we are living in the end times—an era during which the world will be plunged into a series of cataclysmic wars. By the time these wars end, perhaps as much as three-fourths of the earth's population will have died. "Armageddon theology" is the popular designation for biblical prophecies about the end of the world.

In the secular mind such beliefs are little understood. Some people have even gone so far as to accuse evangelical Christians of trying to hasten the end by advocating "a nuclear war as a divine instrument to punish the wicked and complete God's plan for history."[1] These people seem to think that because Christians look forward to the second coming of Christ, they will try to hasten that event, hoping to escape suffering the consequences of Armageddon themselves.

Yet no right-thinking person wants war, no matter what his views of the end times. We all sense the ominous finality of the predictions about the last days and pray that God will stay His hand of judgment. Only an ignorant person could think that humans are clever enough to avoid a final confrontation of disastrous consequences. We may dodge the apocalyptic bullet a few more times, but sooner or later, we will have to face the final moment of history.

DEFINING OUR TERMS

Eschatology is the general term Bible scholars use when they talk about the study of the end times. The term comes from the New Testament Greek word *eschatos,* meaning "last" or "latter." Thus, biblical history moves from a starting point with creation (Genesis 1:1) and progresses toward a final consummation of all things. The Bible itself describes the end like this: "Then the end will come, when he [Christ] hands over the kingdom to God the Father after he has destroyed all dominion, authority and power" (1 Corinthians 15:24).

Several biblical words and phrases describe eschatological events.[2]

Last Days. "Last" and "latter" are adjectives that describe the times just before the end of the age. Paul said, "There will be terrible times in the last days" (2 Timothy 3:1) and, "In the latter times some shall depart from the faith" (1 Timothy 4:1 KJV). Peter said, "In the last days scoffers will come" who deny the promise of Christ's return (2 Peter 3:3).

End of the Age. The "end" (Greek, *telos*) points to the final outcome of all things. Jesus had this in mind when He said, "The end is not yet" (Matthew 24:6 KJV) and "then the end will come" (Matthew 24:14). "Age" (Greek, *aion*) is translated "world" in the King James Version: "the end of the world" (Matthew 24:3). Unfortunately, most people think this refers to the end of the earth, whereas the Greek phrase only means, "the end of the age" (NIV). This term points to a time when the present age will conclude, not the planet itself.

Consummation of the Age. This term (Greek, *sunteleia)* is similar to "end of the age" and expresses the final unfolding of all things. Jesus promises to be with us "to the very end of the age" (Matthew 28:20).

Second Coming. This term does not appear until the writings of the church fathers, but the concept is clearly expressed in the New Testament. It is synonymous with "come back" (John 14:3) and "appear a second time" (Hebrews 9:28). In Greek, the term *parousia* ("coming") describes the arrival and presence of a ruler. *Parousia* is used frequently to describe the coming of Christ (see Matthew 24:3, 27, 37, 39).

Unveiling. "Unveil" or "uncover" (Greek, *apocalupsis*) is the Greek title for the book of Revelation (the Apocalypse). It conveys the idea of a glorious revelation or appearing, as in "you eagerly wait for our Lord Jesus Christ to be revealed" (1 Corinthians 1:7) or "when Jesus Christ is revealed" (1 Peter 1:7).

Appearing. This term (Greek, *epiphaino*) means to "bring to light" or "glorious" and one example of its use appears in the phrase as in "by the splendor of his coming" (2 Thessalonians 2:8). From this term comes the liturgical season of Epiphany, which refers to the coming of Christ.

Day of the Lord. This term and its corollary, the "Day of Christ," refer to the time of final judgment, which culminates with Armageddon, the final battle of all time. It appears in the Old Testament as "that great and dreadful day of the Lord" (Malachi 4:5) and is generally thought to be synonymous with "the time of Jacob's trouble" (Jeremiah 30:7 kjv; *see also* Daniel 12:1). In the New Testament it is "the great day of [Christ's] wrath" (Revelation 6:17).

LOOKING AHEAD

The Tribulation

The Bible clearly warns us that there is coming a time of trouble or tribulation for the whole world. After the seven-sealed scroll described in Revelation 5:1 is opened by Christ (who is the Lamb in Revelation 6:1), the events listed in Revelation 6-19 will take place. For example, Revelation 6:12-14 says:

> There was a great earthquake. The sun turned
> black . . . the whole moon turned blood red, and
> the stars in the sky fell. . . . The sky receded like a
> scroll, rolling up, and every mountain and island
> was removed from its place.

That day will be so terrible that people will beg to die rather
than survive (Revelation 6:16). Scripture goes on to tell us that
as the seven trumpets sounded,

> there came hail and fire mixed with blood. . . . A
> third of the earth was burned up, a third of the
> trees were burned up, and all the green grass was
> burned up. . . . Something like a huge mountain,
> all ablaze, was thrown into the sea. . . . A third of
> the sea turned into blood, a third of the living crea-
> tures in the sea died. . . . A third of the waters
> turned bitter. . . . A third of the day was without
> light (Revelation 8:7-12).

The prophetic record then tells us there will come a great
war in which one-third of mankind will die (Revelation 9:15).
The description of these warring armies defied description by
the writer: "Out of their mouths came fire, smoke and sulfur. . . .
The power . . . was in their mouths . . . their tails were like
snakes" (Revelation 9:17-19). The apostle John had been transported, in the Spirit, down through the canyon of time and the
halls of human history to witness an event so distant in the
future that it was difficult for him to describe what he saw.

Later in Revelation we read about similar disasters associated with the outpouring of the seven bowls of judgment.
Because the various elements of the vision had never been seen
before by John, it was probably hard to comprehend. But today
his description sounds all too familiar—modern warfare, guns,
bombs, even nuclear explosions—a fireball polluting the water
and burning up the surface of the earth. If we are not presently
racing toward this day of the wrath of God, we soon will be.

NAMES OF THE TRIBULATION

The word *tribulation* is derived from the Latin word *tribulum*, which was an agricultural tool used for separating the husks from ears of corn. As found in the Bible, the theological implications would include such concepts as a pressing together, an affliction, a burdening with anguish and trouble, a binding with oppression. Keeping this in mind, it would seem that of all the 12 names for the coming calamity, this one most accurately describes this period.

The "day of the Lord" is the title used more frequently than any other. (*See* Isaiah 2:12; 13:6,9; Ezekiel 13:5; 30:3; Joel 1:15; 2:1,11, 31; 3:14; Amos 5:18,20; Obadiah 15; Zephaniah 1:7,14; Zechariah 14:1; Malachi 4:5; Acts 2:20; 1 Thessalonians 5:2; 2 Thessalonians 2:2; 2 Peter 3:10.) A distinction should be made between the day of the Lord and the day of Christ. The day of Christ is a reference to the millennium.

1. Day of the Lord
2. Tribulation (Matthew 24:21, 29)
3. Indignation (Isaiah 26:20; 34:2)
4. Day of God's vengeance (Isaiah 34:8; 63:1–6)
5. Time of Jacob's trouble (Jeremiah 30:7)
6. Overspreading of abominations (Daniel 9:27)
7. Time of trouble such as never was (Daniel 12:1)
8. Seventieth week (Daniel 9:24–27)
9. Time of the end (Daniel 12:9)
10. Great day of His wrath (Revelation 6:17)
11. Hour of His judgment (Revelation 14:7)
12. End of this world (Matthew 13:40,49)

* Taken from Harold L. Willmington, *The King Is Coming*, Wheaton, IL: Tyndale House, 1991, pp. 58–59. Used with permission.

Babylon the Great

The Book of Revelation speaks at great length in chapters 17-18 about the fall of "Babylon the Great" (Revelation 18:2). This kingdom is personified as "the great whore" (Revelation 17:1 KJV) who has seven heads and ten horns and according to Revelation 17:5 bears the title:

MYSTERY

BABYLON THE GREAT

THE MOTHER OF PROSTITUTES

AND OF THE ABOMINATIONS OF THE EARTH.

This woman is described as "drunk with the blood of the saints . . . who bore testimony to Jesus" (Revelation 17:6). The seven heads are "seven hills on which the woman sits" (Revelation 17:9), and the ten horns are the "ten kings" who are yet to come (Revelation 17:12). The woman herself is "the great city that rules over the kings of the earth" (Revelation 17:18). There is little doubt that John is talking about Rome, the great city that ruled the world of his own day and under whose authority he had been banished to the island of Patmos, where he received this revelation.

The Babylon mentioned in Revelation 17-18 is not the ancient Babylon of Iraq, but rather the center of the great material, economic, and political system of the last days. It is defined as the course of the world's wealth and prosperity. It is the place where sailors and merchants go to make their fortunes (Revelation 18:11-19). Yet there is a final word of judgment spoken against her: "Fallen! Fallen is Babylon the Great! . . . In one hour your doom has come! . . . All your riches and splendor have vanished. . . . In one hour she has been brought to ruin" (Revelation 18:2,10,14,19). Whatever this final act of judgment may be, it is instantaneous, devastating, and permanent. The aftermath certainly seems to describe the consequence of a nuclear war. The prophecy tells of people who watch the "smoke of her burning" from their ships, but they will not go near Babylon—perhaps for fear of contamination.

Identifying the Kingdoms

Not only does the apostle John, the human author of Revelation, make it clear that he is talking about Rome, so also does the Old Testament prophet Daniel. In the days of Nebechadnezzar, king of ancient Babylon, Daniel was taken captive to Babylon in 605 B.C. There he was forced into a training program for the king's service. He was given a Babylonian name, Belteshazzar, and taught "the language and literature of the Babylonians" (Daniel 1:4). While he was still a student in

Five Kingdoms

Gold — BABYLON — Winged Lion

Silver — MEDIA-PERSIA — Lopsided Bear

Brass — GREECE — 4-Winged Leopard

Iron — ROME — 10-Horned Monster with Iron Teeth

Iron & clay — KINGDOM OF ANTICHRIST — Little Horn

training, he had an incredible opportunity to interpret the king's dream about a great statue with a head of gold, arms of silver, belly of brass, legs of iron, and feet of iron and clay. According to the dream, the statue was obliterated by a great rock that filled the whole earth (Daniel 2:31-35).

As Daniel stood before the great Nebuchadnezzar, he told him that God had revealed "what will happen in days to come" (Daniel 2:28). Daniel proceeded to tell Nebuchadnezzar that the king was the head of gold and that after him would arise three other kingdoms inferior to his own. Out of the fourth kingdom would come the ten toes, "partly strong and partly brittle" (Daniel 2:42). "In the time of those kings," Daniel explained, "the God of heaven will set up a kingdom that will never be destroyed . . . but it will itself endure forever" (Daniel 2:44). Notice that the supernatural rock, cut out without hands, struck the ten toes of the statue.

About fifty years later, in 553 B.C., Daniel himself had a vision (Daniel 7) in which he saw "four great beasts" come up from the sea. These beasts represented the same four great empires Nebuchadnezzar saw in his dream. What Nebuchadnezzar saw as a beautiful statue, Daniel saw as wild animals about to tear each other apart!

He saw a winged lion, which symbolized Babylon. Next came a lopsided bear, stronger on one side than the other. He later identified this second kingdom as "Media and Persia" (Daniel 8:20). The two arms of the statue and the lopsided appearance of the bear aptly described the dual empire that would eventually be dominated by Persia. Next, he saw a four-winged leopard, which he later identified as Greece (Daniel 8:21). Finally, he saw a fourth beast with ten horns (Daniel 7:7). Its teeth were iron, the same metal as the fourth kingdom in the statue, and it subdued "whatever was left."

Though this fourth beast is never identified by Daniel, it is clearly Rome, the empire that succeeded Greece. The statue's two legs (Daniel 2:33) seem to indicate the division of Rome into East (Greek-speaking Constantinople) and West (Latin-speaking Rome). The ten horns of this beast parallel the ten toes of the statue (Daniel 2:39-43). They are identified as "ten kings who will come from this kingdom" (Daniel 7:24), after whom will arise "another king," an eleventh king, who will blaspheme God and persecute the saints. Many Bible scholars say this person is the Antichrist.

The Final Empire

Evangelical Christian scholars generally interpret the ten horns of Daniel's fourth beast and the ten toes of the statue as being synonymous. Both grow out of the fourth empire and represent the final phase of it. Amillennialists and postmillennialists view the rock that struck the statue as the *first* coming of Christ. They believe He established His kingdom (the church) back in the days when Rome ruled the world. By contrast, premillennialists see a gap of time, the church age, separating the legs and the toes, with the stone falling at the *second* coming of Christ, during the final stage of Gentile history.

In Nebuchadnezzer's vision, the stone fell on the ten toes and obliterated the statue to dust, the wind blew the dust away, and the stone filled the whole earth. Premillennialists argue that this has not yet happened. They believe this is a prophetic picture of Christ's return to set up His kingdom on earth at the beginning of the Millennium (His 1,000-year reign).

In the meantime, attempts to identify the ten kings pictured by the toes and horns have proven futile. Daniel's vision of the four beasts clearly dates them at the end of time. The "little" horn who rises out of the ten horns (Daniel 7:7-8) is said to continue for "a time (one), times (two) and half a time" (Daniel 7:25), or three and one-half times. This is the same time given for the persecution of the "woman" by the Beast in the Apocalypse (Revelation 12:14; 13:5). This is generally agreed to be the three and one-half years or 42 months of the Great Tribulation (the last half of the seven-year tribulation period).

WHEN WILL THIS HAPPEN?

Daniel's prophecy of the 70 weeks (Daniel 9) tells us that

God put Israel's future on a time clock. God told Daniel that "seventy 'sevens' ('weeks,' KJV) are decreed for your people [Israel] and your holy city [Jerusalem] to finish transgression, to put an end to sin, to atone for wickedness, to bring in everlasting righteousness, to seal up vision and prophecy and to anoint the most holy" (Daniel 9:24).

The prophecy goes on to predict that seven "sevens" will pass as Jerusalem is rebuilt and 62 more "sevens" will pass, for a total of 69, until the Anointed One (Messiah) will be cut off. This leaves one "seven" left for the future. Bible scholars generally interpret these "sevens" (Hebrew, *shabua*) to refer to units of seven years; thus, 70 sevens would equal 490 years. By means of simple calculation, we can determine that the span of time from Artaxerxes' decree for Nehemiah to rebuild Jerusalem to when the Messiah would be cut off (crucified) is 483 years (69 "sevens"). That would bring us to A.D. 32 on the Jewish calendar, which was the year of Christ's crucifixion.[3]

The Jewish calendar was composed of 360 days or twelve months of 30 days. These are the same figures used to calculate that three and one-half years is also 42 months or 1,260 days (Revelation 12:6-14). By following the Jewish calendar, scholars have calculated the beginning date of the Persian Emperor Artaxerxes' decree to send Nehemiah to rebuild the city of Jerusalem (Nehemiah 2:1-9) as Nisan 1 (Jewish calendar) or March 14, 445 B.C. The terminal date would be Nisan 10 (Jewish calendar) or April 6, A.D. 32.

The interval between the decree of Artaxerxes and the triumphal entry of Christ at Jerusalem includes exactly 173,880 days (or 7 x 69 prophetic years of 360 days each). Reckoning the days inclusively according to Jewish practice, Sir Robert Anderson was the first person to work out this computation, and it has been followed by most premillennial scholars.[4] According to Anderson, the 69 weeks of seven years (483 years) ended on the Sunday of our Lord's triumphal entry into Jerusalem; that initiated His final rejection by the Jews, which led to His crucifixion.

Daniel's Seventieth Week

This leaves one "week" or unit of seven years yet to come. Many premillennialists find this final seven years in the tribulation period, which will come after the rapture of the church. During these final seven years, God's prophetic clock for Israel will begin to tick again.

Notice that the prophecy of the "seventy sevens" was given to Daniel in regard to his people (the Jews) and their holy city (Jerusalem). All of the 490 years have to do with *Israel*, not the church. This focuses our attention on the fact that Israel plays a prominent role in the tribulation period.

In the meantime, Daniel was told, "War will continue until the end" (Daniel 9:26). That's what Jesus said in the Olivet Discourse (Matthew 24:6). Thus, we can conclude that the "times of the Gentiles" will be marked by wars and by the rise and fall of the four major empires presented in Daniel chapters 2 and 7.

Then Daniel was told of a ruler ("prince" [Daniel 9:26 KJV]) who was yet to come and "destroy the city and the sanctuary." This ruler will make a covenant (peace treaty) with Israel, then break it in the middle of the seventieth "seven" and turn against Jerusalem and cause "abomination" and "desolation" (Daniel 9:27-28), which Jesus also referred to in His prophetic message (Matthew 24:15).

The Abomination of Desolation

After Daniel's time, the Jews returned to Jerusalem and rebuilt the temple under Zerubbabel and rebuilt the city walls under Nehemiah. Then the Old Testament revelation closed. For nearly 400 "silent years" there was no new revelation from God. Malachi had predicted Elijah would come again to turn people's hearts back to God (Malachi 4:5). And several prophets had pointed to the coming of the Anointed One (Messiah). But as the Old Testament closes, we are left waiting for these promises to be fulfilled.

During the intertestamental period (the silent years), the Jews were severely persecuted by the Seleucid ruler Antiochus IV

Epiphanes. In 168 B.C. he vented his wrath on the Jews, as predicted by Daniel, and desecrated the temple, offering a pig on the holy altar (Daniel 11:21-35). Certainly this was an abomination to the Jews (Daniel 11:31), but notice that it happened *before* the Messiah ever arrived. Soon afterward the Jews revolted under the leadership of Judas Maccabeaus, whose family fought Antiochus' army from 168 to 165 B.C. Their exploits are recorded in the apocryphal books of 1 and 2 Maccabees. After three years of fighting, the Jews were able to restore worship in Jerusalem and they cleansed the temple with a great Feast of Dedication (Hanukkah) on December 25, 165 B.C.[5]

Eventually the Romans conquered Jerusalem and installed Herod the Great as a puppet king under their authority. In an attempt to appease the Jews, Herod had the temple remodeled and greatly expanded. The initial work took about ten years, but construction continued from 20 B.C. to A.D. 64. The edifice was a magnificent sight! Jesus' own disciples were so impressed with it that they called Jesus' attention to the building. But our Lord shocked them when He predicted that the temple would be destroyed and not one stone of it would be left standing (Matthew 24:1-2).

When the Jews revolted against Rome in A.D. 66, the angry Romans decided to retaliate by destroying the temple and burning Jerusalem to the ground. The devastation was carried out in A.D. 70 by Titus, the son of Emperor Vespasian. Jerusalem's occupants were either slaughtered or enslaved. A subsequent revolt in A.D. 135, led by Jesus Bar Kochba, a Jewish zealot, also failed. Hadrian, who was Rome's emperor at the time, had the rubble of Jerusalem plowed under and he erected a Roman city, Aelia Capitolina, from which all Jews were banned. Certainly this was another abomination and desolation.[6]

Over the centuries that followed, either the Romans, the Arabs, or the Crusaders held Jerusalem. The temple was never rebuilt, and the Jews were scattered in the Great Dispersion (*Diaspora*).[7]

Yet Daniel's prophecy looks all the way down the corridor of time "until the end" (Daniel 9:27). He tells us that there is

one great abomination of desolation still on the horizon of the future.

THE KEY PLAYERS

One of the keys to interpreting the prophecies of the end times is found in Revelation 12-13, where seven symbolic people appear. The identity of these people tells us who the major players are in the book of Revelation.

1. *The Woman: Israel* (Revelation 12:1-2,13-16)

The identity of the woman "clothed with the sun . . . and a crown of twelve stars on her head" is the most critical issue in properly interpreting the Apocalypse. The Puritans saw her as the church driven into the wilderness (Revelation 12:14) by the Roman papacy. They viewed the woman as the true church in contrast to the "harlot of Babylon." However, this woman is pregnant with "a male child [Jesus Christ], who will rule all the nations" (Revelation 12:5). The problem with that view is the church did not bring forth Christ; rather, Christ gave birth to the church. The woman, then, has to symbolize Israel because Christ was born of the seed of Israel. Throughout Revelation 12 the woman, the mother of Christ, is persecuted and driven into the wilderness for 1,260 days or three and one-half years (Revelation 12:6,14) and suffers great tribulation—the "time of Jacob's [Israel's] trouble." Amillennialists who see no future for national Israel are forced to view the woman as the church, but she is not. Scripture presents her as the mother of Christ (Israel), not the bride of Christ (the church).

2. *The Dragon: Satan* (Revelation 12:3-4; 9-13)

The "enormous red dragon with seven heads and ten horns" (Revelation 12:3) is identified as "the devil, or Satan" (Revelation 12:9). He is called the "accuser of our brothers, who accuses them before our God day and night" (verse 10). This description is reminiscent of Satan's activity in the book of Job. Verse 4 describes Satan as the one who tried to devour the child as soon as it was born. The whole passage reminds us of the great spiritual warfare going on behind the scenes of human history.

3. *The Male Child: Christ* (Revelation 12:2,5)

The child is Jesus Christ, who will "rule all the nations with an iron scepter" (Revelation 12:5). His being "snatched up" to the throne of God refers to Christ's ascension back to heaven (Acts 1:9-11). Jesus is symbolized as a Lamb in Revelation 5, 14, 19, 21-22.[8] He is the one who will open the seven-sealed scroll, which is the title deed to the universe. He is the one who will gather His elect and judge the unbelieving world. He is the Bridegroom at the wedding supper in Revelation 19:7-9. He is the rider on the white horse who overcomes the Beast, the False Prophet, and the dragon and rules forever.

4. *The Michael: The Archangel* (Revelation 12:7-12)

In this spectacular prophecy, we are told that Michael and his angels will cast Satan out of heaven. Lucifer (or Satan) has already "fallen" from his lofty position, but he still has access to the throne of God (see Job 1:6-12; 2:1-7). But here we see Satan booted out of heaven completely. He is angry because he knows his time is short (Revelation 12:12), so he vents his anger on the woman (Israel), who had given birth to the child. His time left is "a time, times and half a time," or three and one-half years (Revelation 12:14). This time coincides with the last half of Daniel's seventieth week, the Great Tribulation.

5. *The Remnant: Believers* (Revelation 12:17)

When Satan is thwarted in his attempt to destroy national Israel, he will turn against the remnant of her seed

PERSONALITIES OF THE TRIBULATION

ᐁᐁᐁ   ᐁᐁᐁ   ᐁᐁᐁ

Prophecy of the end times is a program of the world's most sobering drama, introducing the cast of a fantastic play. And Christians have the great confidence of knowing the final outcome—that the Lord Jesus Christ will triumph over His enemies and live forever in glorious eternity with His children.

1. The Holy Spirit
2. The Devil (Revelation 12:12)
3. Two special Old Testament witnesses (**Revelation 11:3**)
4. The Antichrist (2 Thessalonians 2:3-4,9)
5. The False Prophet (Revelation 13:11)
6. A multitude of specialized angels
7. 144,000 Israelite preachers (Revelation 7:4)
8. An army of locust-like demons from the bottomless pit (Revelation 9:2-3)
9. An army of horse and rider demons from the Euphrates River (Revelation 9:16)
10. Three evil spirits (Revelation 16:13-14)
11. A cruel, power-mad ruler from the north (Ezekiel 38:1-3)
12. Four symbolic women
    a. A persecuted woman (Israel) (Revelation 12:1)
    b. A vile and bloody harlot (the false church) (Revelation 17:3-5)
    c. An arrogant queen (the world's political and economic systems) (Revelation 18:2,7)
    d. A pure, chaste bride (the true church) (Revelation 19:7-8)
13. A mighty warrior from heaven (Revelation 19:11,16)

---

* Taken with permission from Harold L. Willmington, *The King Is Coming*, Wheaton, IL: Tyndale House, 1991, pp. 72-75.

who have the "testimony of Jesus." These are converted Jews who will have come to faith in Jesus as their Messiah. They will be persecuted severely by the two beasts that are forthcoming. Some people speculate that the deliverance by the "wings of a great eagle" (Revelation 12:14) may refer to an airlift, but that is purely speculation.

6. *The Beast of the Sea: Antichrist* (Revelation 13:1-10)

This creature represents the epitome and culmination of the Gentile powers of all time. Thus, he resembles a lion, a bear, and a leopard, as in Daniel's vision of the four beasts (Daniel 7). He is also symbolized by seven heads and ten horns, as in Daniel's prophecy of the fourth beast, or fourth empire. This creature is said to "blaspheme God," to make "war against the saints," and receive "worship" from unbelievers. The apostle Paul calls him the "man of lawlessness" (2 Thessalonians 2:3) or "man of sin" (KJV) or "son of perdition" (KJV), who will "exalt himself over everything that is called God or is worshiped, so that he sets himself up in God's temple, proclaiming himself to be God" (2 Thessalonians 2:4).

Most Bible commentators understand the Beast of the sea to be the Antichrist. Whether he is a specific person, a political system, or both is a matter of debate. Since he is associated with the same symbol given to Rome (seven heads and ten horns), it is assumed that he represents the revived Roman Empire of the last days. Some people speculate this could be in the process of being formed even now in the European Economic Community (EEC).

The characteristics of this beast are the same as those of the little horn of Daniel's prophecy (Daniel 7:8). He also appears to be the "ruler" or "prince" (KJV) who will bring the final abomination of desolation upon Jerusalem.

7. *The Beast of the Earth: False Prophet* (Revelation 13:11-18)

This creature is distinct from the Beast of the sea;

notice that he calls attention to the first Beast and persuades the world to worship the Antichrist. He even sets up an "image" of the first Beast "so that it could speak" (Revelation 13:15). The speculative possibilities here are endless. Is this some kind of televised image? Can this telecast accommodate two-way communication? Is it a projected holographic image that actually appears as a three-dimensional person? At this point in time, no one knows for sure.

In Revelation 13:16 we see that the second Beast will force people to receive the mark of the first Beast which is described as "a mark [insignia or logo], which is the name of the Beast or the number of his name. . . . His number is 666" (Revelation 13:17-18). Without this number, people cannot buy or sell.

Whoever or whatever this second Beast is, he is able to control the world politically, religiously, and economically during the tribulation period. Later, when these two Beasts are conquered by Jesus Christ and cast into the lake of fire, they are called "the beast" and "the false prophet" (Revelation 19:20). Many people believe these two Beasts will comprise the one-world government and religion of the last days.

How Can We Be Sure?

Since much of the interpretation of prophecy rests on the symbolism found in Daniel and Revelation, we need to be cautious about assuming that our own views are right and speculating beyond what the Scripture actually states as fact.

We all would like to think that our view is the correct view of prophecy, but we must remember that among genuine believers there will be differences on matters of eschatology. Unfortunately, we all too often fail to focus on the issues alone and attack our opponents personally. When we stoop to condemning a fellow believer for being different or attack his character and sincerity, we are really admitting our insecurity about our own position.

Tragically, eschatology has become a divisive subject among evangelicals. In some circles, any variation from commonly held views results in immediate expulsion, ostracism, and denunciation. This keeps many church leaders from any healthy discussion about the end times or evaluation of other eschatological options. Because people are usually reluctant to question their leaders, there has come a great stagnation in the whole area of eschatology in recent years. What's worse is that some people are completely unaware of other options and keep preaching or passing on what they have been taught as though it were fact.

As a premillennialist, I have certain prejudices in my own views about eschatology. I believe the postmillennial dream of bringing in the kingdom of Christ on earth during the church age is a futile enterprise. But that does not mean that postmillennialists are to be shunned. There are postmillennialists who have made a significant impact on society and Christendom. Jonathan Edwards, the Puritan revivalist, was a postmillennialist, and he is revered in all evangelical circles. So are great postmillennial theologians like Charles Hodge and Benjamin Warfield.

I believe amillennialists fail to distinguish between Israel and the church and I don't agree with the way they allegorize the prediction of a 1,000-year kingdom on earth. But this does not make them Christ-denying heretics. They are to be commended for their concern that the church fulfill its responsibilities on earth and prepare men and women for the judgment to come. Prominent amillennialists include television pastor D. James Kennedy, the founder of Evangelism Explosion, and biblical counseling advocate Jay Adams. Both of these men have made great contributions to the cause of the evangelical faith, as have amillennial scholars such as William Hendriksen and Anthony Hoekema.

American Christianity has a rich, varied heritage of eschatological teaching that is virtually absent in England, continental Europe, and other parts of the world. We have an opportunity to benefit from each other's perspectives if we are willing to discuss and evaluate our beliefs based upon the facts of prophetic Scripture. Indeed, that is our endeavor in the upcoming chapters of *Final Signs*.

Chapter 2

ᐸᗩᗩᐳ

SEPARATING FACT FROM FICTION IN BIBLE PROPHECY

Most of us would like to believe that Jesus is coming in our lifetime. Yet even as we anticipate the Lord's return, we need to be aware that eschatological excitement and prophetic panic tend to go hand in hand. Every time a war heats up in the Middle East there are a number of "prophetic panhandlers" who assure us that this is the Big One. Despite the church's twenty-century-long struggle to understand biblical prophecy, these modern-day "prophets" claim to have the last days and Christ's return all figured out—some to the very day!

One Saturday afternoon my telephone rang. I was drinking a cup of coffee and contemplating mowing the grass when the disruption came. On the phone was a preacher friend of mine in California; he was all excited about the rapture happening soon.

"I've just read the most amazing booklet about Bible prophecy!" Randy shouted all the way from the West coast. "This guy has calculated the events of the end times and predicts the rapture will occur on September 12, 1988!"

"You've got to be kidding!" I responded. "Those things never work out the way they claim."

"No, this is for real," Randy insisted. "This guy is an engineer and he has spent years working out a detailed calculation based on the Feast of Trumpets [Rosh Hashanah] symbolizing the rapture."

"I've heard that before," I said. "Some people were saying that back in 1975 and nothing happened. Who is this writer?" I asked.

Randy paused a moment while he scanned the cover of the booklet. "Edgar Whisenant," he stated somewhat cautiously. "The booklet is entitled, *88 Reasons Why the Rapture Will Be in 1988.*"[1]

"I've never heard of him!" I said sternly, as though I expected my voice to indicate some sense of authority and finality. After a few silent seconds, I asked, "Where did you get this booklet?"

"It came in the mail," Randy explained jubilantly. "Everybody is talking about it out here."

"Well, nobody in St. Louis knows anything about it," I assured him.

"Don't you think it's possible that he's right?" Randy asked, pleading for some reasonable consideration on my part.

"Randy, you used to be one of my students," I replied. "Remember, just because something is possible doesn't mean it is probable. It is possible that the moon may disappear, but it isn't probable that it will."

Randy's enthusiasm is typical of many evangelical Christians today. They sincerely believe the Bible, but they also want to make it say more than it really says. They want to believe that they are living in the last days and that the events of this era have great prophetic significance. The problem is that Christians have had that mindset for centuries and have often attempted to read prophecy through the eyes of their own experiences. The results have been a host of miscalculated guesses based on faulty presuppositions.

Now, there's nothing wrong with evangelical Christians taking seriously the doctrine of the second coming of Christ. Scripture says that He will literally return to the earth one day to vindicate the church and judge the world. We may differ among ourselves on *when* and *how* He will return, but most of us are convinced He will return as He promised.

However, we must exercise discernment when we deal with the imminence of Christ's return. Most of us believe that He could come at any moment. There are exceptions to this, of course, but most evangelical Christians are expecting Him to come soon. While this hope gives the church great comfort and expectation, it often leads to excessive speculation. Think of all the "candidates" for Antichrist that have been proposed in the twentieth century alone.

EVERYTHING OLD IS NEW AGAIN

Suddenly a thought hit me. "Randy," I said, "how long have you been a Christian?"

"Ten years," he answered, sounding somewhat bewildered.

"That's the problem!" I announced. "You haven't been in Christian circles long enough to have heard of past surefire predictions that have misfired. You don't have the perspective to evaluate this kind of conjecture."

At that moment, I realized why some Christians are so quick to accept such predictions without question. They just don't know any better. Many of them have only a limited knowledge of biblical prophecy. In most cases they believe whatever end-times position is taken in the church where they were converted. "After all," they theorize, "if our church is right about salvation, we must be right about prophecy too." Even pastors with theological training have been known to fall for some of the latest eschatological scams.

I have been somewhat surprised that only a few words of caution have been raised to warn Christians about end times confusion. To the contrary, new date-setters have come and gone. A Korean sect took out newspaper ads predicting October 22, 1992. Long-time radio Bible teacher Harold Camping suggested 1994.[2] Undoubtedly as we approach A.D. 2000, more suggestions will be forthcoming.

At least one prophecy "expert" has insisted that the rapture has to happen before A.D. 2000 in order to culminate 6,000 years of human history before the 1,000-year millennial kingdom is established, which would bring us to a grand total of 7,000 years in the divine plan of the ages. This idea has been around for centuries. The Talmud ascribes it to the "School of Elijah." Martin Luther and Phillip Melancthon quoted it during the Reformation.[3] But the idea has no real basis or support in Scripture. It is merely based on the false assumption that God has limited human history to 6,000 years.

This theory may sound like a clever arrangement of biblical numerics. But it will soon be proven wrong. If Jesus Christ does not return before the year 2000, this scheme will have to be abandoned altogether. But this need not alarm us because this scheme was never clearly taught in Scripture in the first place!

VIEWING PROPHECY THROUGH OUR OWN EYES

Perhaps the church's greatest problem with interpreting biblical prophecy is the desire to view it through personal experience. The German theologians call this a *zeitgeist,* a current mood or response to certain existing conditions. Unfortunately, as we have seen in this brief history of eschatological speculation, this has happened more often than not. The great temptation in prophetic interpretation is to move from the *facts* to our own *assumptions* and *speculations.*

The twentieth century is loaded with examples of prophetic speculations that never came true. Many people have assumed that ours must be the last age and that in the last days the Antichrist will form an alliance of European nations and attack Israel. Here is just a sample of the proposals that have been offered:

1. *Kaiser Wilhelm*

   The German emperor's title meant "Caesar," and he intended to conquer all of Europe and reunite the old Roman Empire. Even the popular American evangelist Billy Sunday bought into this idea that Wilhelm was the Antichrist, often stating: "If you turn hell upside down, you'll find 'Made in Germany' stamped on the bottom!" During World War I, the Kaiser was the most likely candidate for the Antichrist.

2. *Benito Mussolini*

   The Italian strongman from Rome rose to power in Europe after World War I, and prophetic speculators tagged him as the Antichrist long before World War II began. After all, they reasoned, Mussolini is in Rome and wants to revive the Roman Empire; therefore, he will join hands with the people and rule the world.

3. *Adolph Hitler*

   Hitler has come to be the ultimate personification of evil. What better candidate for the Antichrist? He persecuted and murdered six million Jews and tried to conquer all of Europe. He formed a murderous alliance with Mussolini and turned his hand against everyone. Eventually, they were both destroyed.

4. *Joseph Stalin*

   This atheistic leader of the Soviet Union may have been our ally during World War II, but it was an uneasy alliance at best. Some American prophecy buffs had him tagged as the "man of sin" long before and after Hitler. After all, they suggested, Russia is the Magog of Ezekiel's prophecy (Ezekiel 38-39).

5. *Nikita Khrushchev*

Many people still remember the outspoken, shoe-pounding, large, bald man of the Soviet Union from his violent speech at the United Nations in which he threatened to bury us all. Some Christians speculated that he could be the Antichrist. But they were wrong.

6. *John F. Kennedy*

Believe it or not, anti-Catholic fundamentalists in the early 1960s believed Kennedy was the top candidate for becoming the Antichrist. They were sure he was going to deceive and take over the world by forming an alliance with the pope, black people, and communists.

7. *Mikhail Gorbachev*

Christians were once nervous about Gorbachev. He seemed too good to be true with his *perestroika* and *glasnost* offers of peace and his plan to hold the balance of power in check with his nuclear arsenal. People have asked me if the mark on his head might be the "mark of the Beast"!

8. *Ronald Wilson Reagan*

Yes, even the darling of the New Right and practically the entire evangelical Christian church was targeted as a candidate for Antichrist because his three names each contain six letters, which some people connected with the number 666.

9. *Saddam Hussein*

Some people have suggested Hussein will sign a peace treaty with Israel only to break it later and renew his hostilities toward the Promised Land.

10. *Bill Clinton*

Some people believe Clinton is the Antichrist and Al Gore is the False Prophet of New Age nature religion. Another scenario has Bill Clinton as the Antichrist and Hillary as the False Prophet.

Other candidates have included Henry Kissinger, Margaret Thatcher, Boris Yeltsin, and even George Bush. The problem with these identifications is that they are always tentative and viewed through the *zeitgeist* of our own times. Identifications that now seem ludicrous once held great popular appeal.

The real tragedy is that instead of rejecting prophetic speculation for what it is, we are often duped by it. People guessing dates and selecting candidates for the Antichrist are claiming to know more than the writers of Scripture, and that is always dangerous. Dr. Daniel Mitchell writes, "Speculating on the date of Christ's return not only breeds bad theology, but it is the original sin all over again—trying to know as much as God."[4] He goes on to note that the expectation of Christ's return *at any moment* has been a source of hope and comfort to the church since the days of the apostles. Any apparent delay is due not to God's indecision, but to the fact that He has not let us in on the secret!

I believe the Bible clearly predicts the rise of a personal Antichrist at the end of human history, but I doubt we will ever know who he is until it is too late. The apostle Paul said of him, "Don't let anyone deceive you in any way, for that day will not come until the rebellion occurs and the man of lawlessness ["man of sin" KJV] is revealed, the man doomed to destruction" (2 Thessalonians 2:3). Paul reminds us that the "power of lawlessness" (2 Thessalonians 2:7) is already at work, but it will eventually culminate when the lawless one is revealed (2 Thessalonians 2:8).

In the meantime, we are admonished to "stand firm" and hold to the doctrine of the apostles of our Lord (2 Thessalonians 2:15) that we might be strengthened "in every good deed and word" (2 Thessalonians 2:17). Thus, Paul's advice to us is the same as that of the Lord Jesus, who told us to watch, stay ready, and keep serving until He comes (Matthew 24:42-46).

Here is a key principle to keep in mind at all times: When you study the *facts* of prophecy, be sure that you distinguish them from the *assumptions* you draw of the *speculations* you make. While we would all like to believe that our Lord will come in our lifetime, it is presumptuous to assume that we are the terminal generation. Surely He could come today, but then again He may not come for many years. That decision is up to God the Father.

GUIDELINES FOR UNDERSTANDING PROPHECY

Finding your way through the maze of traffic in a major city can be difficult—especially if you don't know where you are going. It's not only challenging, it can even be dangerous.

Some people view Bible prophecy the same way. It looks like a hopeless maze of eschatological confusion. So they throw up their hands in defeat. "I just can't make any sense out of this!" they exclaim in frustration.

One of the most difficult tasks in interpreting God's Word has been that of discerning the prophecies of the end times. First, we must remember that the people of Jesus' day missed many of the predictions of His first coming. Therefore, we must not presume that we have figured out all the details of His second coming. Second, we must guard against the great temptation to read prophecy through the eyes of the present. This has been a problem throughout church history. As early as the second century A.D., believers have speculated about the time and place of the Lord's return.

Unfortunately, unguarded speculation has often prevailed as the most popular approach to biblical prophecy. Some of the wildest possible scenarios have received the most incredible popular support. In a few cases, prophecy even became the tool with which a person could justify himself and condemn his critics.

Every imaginable speculation has arisen as to the identity of the Antichrist, the date of the rapture, and the beginning of the Battle of Armageddon. In our effort to make sense of all this, let me suggest a simple paradigm:

Facts. There are the clearly stated facts of prophetic revelation: Christ will return for His own; He will judge the world; there will be a time of great trouble on the earth at the end of the age; the final conflict will be won by Christ; and so on. These basic facts are clearly stated in Scripture.

Assumptions. Factual prophecy only tells us so much and no more. Beyond that we must make certain assumptions. If these are correct, they will lead to valid conclusions, but if not, they may lead to ridiculous speculations. For example, it is an assumption that Russia will invade Israel in the last days. Whether or not that is factual depends on the legitimacy of one's interpretation of Ezekiel's Magog prophecy (Ezekiel 38-39). It is foolish to say we don't need to worry about Russia because it will be destroyed. That is only an assumption.

Speculations. These are purely calculated guesses based on assumptions. In many cases they have no basis in prophetic fact at all. For example, the Bible says the number of the Antichrist is "666" (Revelation 13:18). We must try to assume what this means. It is an assumption that it is a literal number that will appear on things in the last days. When one prominent evangelist saw the number 666 prefixed on automobile license plates in Israel a few years ago, he speculated the "mark of the Beast" had already arrived in the Holy Land.

The greatest danger of all in trying to interpret biblical prophecy is to assume that our speculations are true and preach them as facts.[5] This has often caused great embarrassment and confusion. For example, when Benito Mussolini rose to power in Rome in the 1920s, many Christians assumed he might be the Antichrist, who would rule the world from the city of seven hills in the last days. Some even speculated that Adolph Hitler, who rose to power later in Germany, was the False Prophet. Others were sure the False Prophet was the pope, who was also in Rome.

The time has come when serious students of biblical prophecy must be clear about what is fact, what is assumption, and what is speculation. For example, just because a war breaks out in the Middle East does not mean that war will necessarily lead to Armageddon. Just because modern geopolitical Iraq includes the ruins of ancient Babylon does not necessarily mean that Iraq will be the Babylon of the last days.

I recently heard someone say that Baghdad will be destroyed and Babylon will be rebuilt as the capital of Iraq and eventually it will become the new home of the United Nations. That is pure speculation! It assumes that prophetic Babylon is Iraq, then speculates that Babylon will be rebuilt and that the United Nations will move there to set up one world government.

Anything is possible, but that does not mean something is probable. The Babylon described in Revelation 17-18 sounds, in some ways, more like the United States of Europe than Iraq. Both the United States and Europe are rich and prosperous, yet immoral and corrupt at the same time. Remember, Babylon is described as a place where merchants go by ship (Revelation 18:17) to buy their goods and materials: gold, silver, jewelry, clothing, perfumes, and food. Yet in one hour, this great place will be destroyed (Revelation 18:19).

The issue at stake is not whether Babylon is the United States, Europe, or Iraq, or whether Magog is Russia or Iran, or even whether the Antichrist is a person or a system (or both). The issue at stake is that we must carefully distinguish between the *facts* of prophecy and our own *assumptions* and *speculations*.

The greatest *fact* of all is that we who are in Christ have the hope of eternal life. The apostle Peter said, "In his great mercy he has given us new birth into a living hope . . . into an inheritance that can never perish, spoil or fade—kept in heaven for you . . . ready to be revealed in the last time" (1 Peter 1:3-5).

A VARIETY OF VIEWS

One of the unique and complex features of biblical prophecy is that it may be interpreted by different hermeneutical models. Within the Christian church there have been a variety of approaches to the study of eschatology, or the last days. Liberal Protestants refuse to consider prophecy at all, preferring to dismiss it as hopelessly confusing or generally irrelevant. But among evangelical Christians, prophecy has always been taken seriously. Jesus Christ Himself predicted His return to earth as well as several significant end-time events (Matthew 24-25).

The issue at stake among evangelicals has generally involved *how* a person interprets prophecy.[6] Three main schools of thought have been proposed. While most evangelical Christians are premillennialists in their view of eschatology, some are also amillennial or postmillennial.

Postmillennial. This school of thought believes that the Millennium (the 1,000-year reign of Christ mentioned in Revelation 20:1-3, 6-7) is to be interpreted symbolically as synonymous with the church age. Satan's power is viewed as being "bound" by the power of the gospel. Postmillennialists believe that during this Millennium (church age) the church is called upon to conquer unbelief, convert the masses, and govern society by the mandate of biblical law. Only after Christianity succeeds on earth will Christ return and announce that His kingdom has been realized. Postmillennial advocates have included Catholics, Puritans, charismatics, and dominionists who urge believers to take dominion over the earth and its political governments in order to usher in the kingdom of God on earth.[7]

Amillennial. This approach sees no Millennium of any kind on the earth. Rather, amillennialists tend to view so-called millennial prophecies as being fulfilled in eternity. Biblical references to the "thousand years" are interpreted symbolically. In this scheme the church age ends with the return of Christ to judge the world and usher in eternity. God's promises to Israel are viewed as having been fulfilled in the church (the New Israel of the new covenant); therefore, amillennialists see no specific future for national Israel. They view the church age as an era of conflict between the forces of good and evil, which culminates with the return of Christ.[8]

Premillennial. This view says that Christ will return at the end of the church age to set up His kingdom on earth for a literal 1,000 years.[9] Most premillennialists also believe there will be a period of great tribulation on earth prior to the return of

Christ. Some premillennialists believe the church will go through the Tribulation (post-Tribulationists), others believe the church will be raptured prior to the Tribulation (pre-Tribulationists), and a small number believe the church will be raptured in the middle of the Tribulation (mid-Tribulationists).[10] Despite these differences in regard to the rapture of the church, premillennialists generally believe in the future restoration of the state of Israel and the eventual conversion of the Jews to Christianity.

Most evangelical Christians hold to the dispensational premillennial view of eschatology, which looks forward to the rapture ("translation" or "absorption" of believers to heaven) as the next major prophetic event. This, they believe, will end the church age and prepare the way for the Tribulation and the return of Christ. One Bible passage that suggests the rapture is 1 Thessalonians 4:16-17: "The Lord Himself will come down from heaven, with a loud command, with the voice of the archangel and with the trumpet call of God, and the dead in Christ will rise first. After that, we who are still alive and are left will be caught up together with them in the clouds to meet the Lord in the air. And so we will be with the Lord forever."

Commenting on the rapture of the church, David Jeremiah writes: "When Jesus Christ returns for His own, the world will not hear the voice nor the trumpet. The ears of nonbelievers will be deaf and their eyes blind. It will take place so fast, 'in the twinkling of an eye,' that no one left behind will understand what has happened."[11]

TAKING PROPHECY SERIOUSLY

Whatever a person's eschatological preference may be, evangelical Christians take seriously the Bible prophecies about the end times, the Great Tribulation, Armageddon, and the return of Christ. In fact, we are genuinely convinced that the march to Armageddon, the last great battle, has already begun. Many Christians believe we are living in the end times—when the world will be plunged into a series of cataclysmic wars that

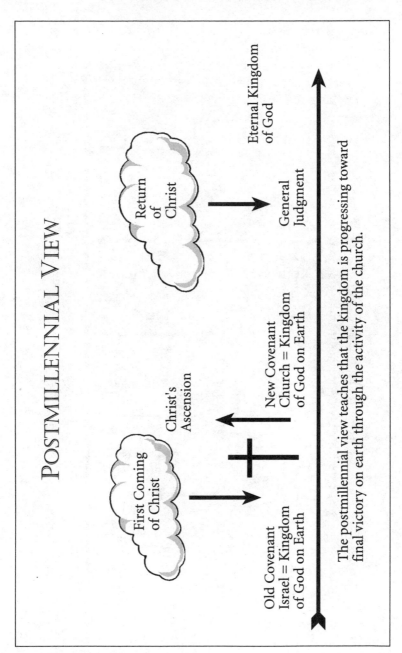

Postmillennial View

First Coming of Christ

Christ's Ascension

Old Covenant
Israel = Kingdom
of God on Earth

New Covenant
Church = Kingdom
of God on Earth

Return of Christ

General Judgment

Eternal Kingdom of God

The postmillennial view teaches that the kingdom is progressing toward final victory on earth through the activity of the church.

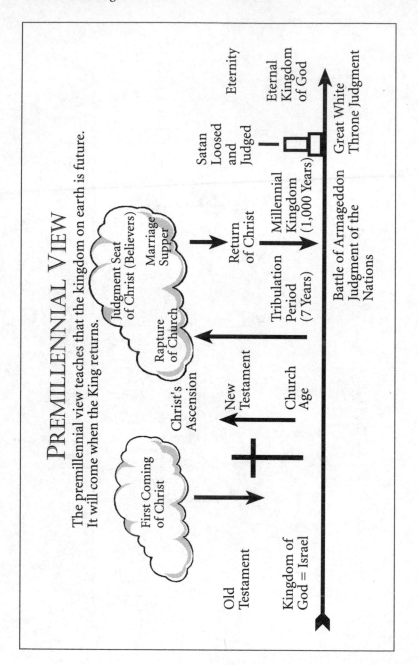

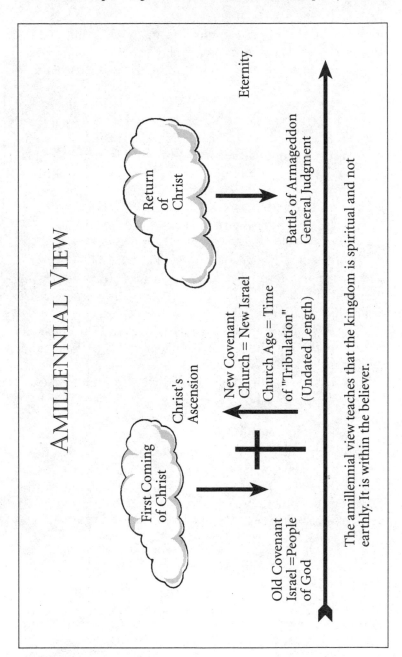

AMILLENNIAL VIEW

Return
of
Christ

Eternity

Battle of Armageddon
General Judgment

New Covenant
Church = New Israel

Church Age = Time
of "Tribulation"
(Undated Length)

Christ's
Ascension

First Coming
of Christ

Old Covenant
Israel =People
of God

The amillennial view teaches that the kingdom is spiritual and not earthly. It is within the believer.

may well claim three-fourths of the world's population. However, just because evangelical Christians believe such prophecies does not mean they want to hasten these events.

In recent years, more and more of the secular community has come to agree that we seem to be approaching the end of the world. Nobel laureates and reputable scientists have warned that the earth's time clock is running out. Air and water pollution, the evaporation of the protective ozone layer, the elimination of oxygen-producing rain forests, and the general instability of the earth's crust have all been cited as serious problems that could hinder the future of life on this planet.

In past centuries, when Christians talked about the end of the world, people often laughed at them because the destruction of the entire planet was simply inconceivable. But today, both Christians and agnostics realize it is well within the realm of possibility. The gloomy apocalyptic vision of Jonathan Schell's *Fate of the Earth* is an example of such concern.[12]

The Bible warns us that the "day of the Lord will come like a thief in the night" (1 Thessalonians 5:1-2). It will be an instantaneous event that will catch the world unprepared. In fact, the Bible reminds us that people will promise, "'Peace, peace'...when there is no peace" (Jeremiah 8:11; *see also* Ezekiel 13:10).

Mankind has demonstrated irrevocably that it cannot bring a permanent and lasting peace to this world. Every human effort at peace has been short-lived and destined to failure. At the end of time, when the stakes are the highest, the greatest gamble for peace ever made will end in the greatest battle of all time—at Armageddon.

Is There Any Hope?

Nearly 2,000 years have passed since Jesus promised, "I will come back" (John 14:3). Throughout the subsequent generations of church history, believers have held tenaciously to this promise. It has become to the church what the apostle Paul called "that blessed hope, and the glorious appearing of the great God and our Savior Jesus Christ" (Titus 2:13 KJV).

Behind the facts of history, Christians see a great spiritual conflict with the powers of darkness.[13] God has clearly been at work in human history, but so has Satan. Humankind has produced its saints and its sinners, its Florence Nightingales and its Adolph Hitlers. Secular history views this as a mere process of natural selection. By contrast, sacred history views God as sovereign over the natural process. Christianity begins with the presupposition that God is at work in history. In fact, Christianity teaches that God has already intervened in human history and will continue to do so in the future.

Each social transition has thrust humanity into a new era of human experience. In each transition, the old social order seemed to fade away as it was replaced by a new social order. Many people believe that we are now on the brink of such a transition again—this time to a global world order.

One economy, a global economy, will soon replace our diverse national economies. One government, an international cooperative body, will overshadow individual governments— even our own. Finally, one religion, an apostate form of pseudo-Christianity, will unite the religious world. There may be pockets of exceptions here and there—a few evangelicals, the Muslims, and certainly the Jews. But the prophecies of the end times indicate they will come under persecution by the leader of the world system.

Modern man has reached the point in his intellectual journey where he does not want to face the logical consequences of a secular world without God. But instead of turning to God, people are now turning to a kind of scientific mysticism that has been popularized as the New Age movement. This trendy new approach to religion without rules combines transcendentalism, spiritualism, Oriental mysticism, and transpersonal psychology.

In the meantime, the storm that is gathering on the human horizon looks more ominous all the time. The instability of the world economy has business leaders worried all over the world.

The realignment of nations on the European continent leaves many questions still unanswered about the future of Europe. The continued strife in the Middle East unnerves us all, for it is a constant reminder of how quickly the march to Armageddon could begin.

Chapter 3

⁖𝍢𝍣⁖

Signs of
the End Times

Questions about the second coming of Christ and the end of the world are not new. Jesus' own disciples raised three such questions themselves. In Matthew 24-25 we find Jesus' answer to these questions. In fact, these chapters contain Jesus' last major discourse and His clearest statements about the future. His message included a prediction of the imminent fall of Jerusalem and also pointed to the distant future when "the times of the Gentiles" would come to an end during the Great Tribulation.

The discourse began when the disciples expressed their awe of the spectacular architecture of the temple. To their amazement, Jesus replied that "not one stone here will be left on another; every one will be thrown down" (Matthew 24:2). Stunned by this remark, the disciples asked their Lord three questions in the next verse:

1. "When will this happen?"
2. "What will be the sign of Your coming?"
3. "What will be the sign of the end of the age?"

As He sat on the Mount of Olives opposite the temple precincts, Jesus answered those questions in what is commonly referred to as the Olivet Discourse. His entire message in Matthew 24-25 is the answer to these three questions. John Walvoord comments, "Premillenarians, accordingly, interpret the discourse as an accurate statement of end-time events, which will lead up to and climax in the second coming of Christ to set up His millennial kingdom on earth."[1]

The key to interpreting this passage rests in a person's view of the "gospel of the kingdom" (Matthew 14:13-14). Since Matthew has already shown in his parables that the present form of the kingdom is the church, it seems proper to interpret the events in this discourse as encompassing the entire church age and culminating dramatically toward the end of that age. Therefore, the apostle John could say in Revelation 1:9 that he was a "companion in tribulation, and in the kingdom" even though he was still in the church age. Thus, the "signs" (Greek, *semeion*) of the end are general characteristics of the present age, and they will increase in intensity as this age moves toward its conclusion. These are followed by more specific signs (Matthew 24:15-26) of the tribulation period and the final return of Christ in judgment (Matthew 24:27-31).

A Call to Discernment

Jesus warned His followers not to be deceived by the large parade of false prophets and messiahs who would surface throughout the church age. He also warned of "wars and rumors of wars" (Matthew 24:6) that have continually marked the age of the Gentiles and would follow throughout the present era. Such wars do *not* in themselves indicate that the end is near. These are only the "beginning of birth pains" (Matthew 24:8). These conflicts may point to the end, but serious Bible students dare not interpret any one conflict as necessarily "prophetic" of the end times. In reality, every war that occurs on earth during this present era is a fulfillment of our Lord's prophecy.

Despite such wars, Jesus warned in Matthew 24:6, "The end is still to come" ("the end is not yet" [KJV]). Unfortunately, some people miss this point altogether. They read about wars, earthquakes, and natural disasters and conclude that the end must be near. Yet Jesus Himself said such is not the case.

Thus the recent Persian Gulf War cannot be viewed as a fulfillment of prophecy in itself, though it may be a step in that direction. This is precisely where Bible students need to be careful not to jump from the facts of prophecy to their well-intended assumptions and, ultimately, their speculations.

Every type of event listed in this part of Jesus' response—wars, famines, and earthquakes—is to be expected throughout the church age until He returns. These are the "beginning of birth pains" (Matthew 24:8), but they do not in themselves prove the final fulfillment is about to be delivered.

Every major crisis in the Middle East—those that took place in 1948, 1956, 1967, 1973, and 1991—has led to similar prophetic speculations with sincere teachers announcing that the end is just around the corner. What the most recent crises show is that the old animosities have not died out and the potential for a major Arab alliance against Israel is still a very real possibility in the future—but that future and the accompanying last days could be a month, a year, ten years, or even a hundred years from now.

THE END OF THE AGE

Jesus stated that the end of the age would come when the "gospel of the kingdom" has been preached "in the whole world as a testimony to all nations" (Matthew 24:14). He did not clearly define whether this proclamation of the gospel is *announced* to all the world (Greek, *oikoumene,* "inhabited world") and every nation (Greek, *ethnos,* "Gentile nations") or *believed* in every nation. But one fact is clear: Christ's great commission to evangelize the world (Matthew 28:18-20) is to be carried out faithfully until He returns. Christ's later warning that no one knows the time of His return (Matthew 24:36) emphasizes that we are to continue doing what He commanded until He comes.

The end (Greek, *telos*) that will come after the proclamation of the gospel is the end of the church age, which parallels "the times of the Gentiles" during the present era. While some commentators limit the events in Matthew 24 to the tribulation period, it seems clear that they are occurring throughout the entire church age as the gospel is preached primarily to the Gentiles.[2]

It is important to note that Jesus spoke of the "end of the *age*" in response to His disciples' questions. There can be no doubt that He viewed human history as moving toward a final climax rather then in an endless cycle of repetitious events. William S. LaSor notes that the Jews of the intertestamental period distinguished between "this age" (Hebrew, *hauolam hazzeh*) and "the age to come" (Hebrew, *hauolam habbah*). Thus, LaSor concludes that the expression "the end of the world" comes from Judeo-Christian roots and is understood by both Jews and Christians as referring to this world (or age) coming to an end and being replaced by the age to come.[3]

A similar concept is found in the Old Testament expression "the latter days" (Hebrew, *beaharit hayyamim*). Moses foretold the future apostasy of Israel, her scattering, and her return to the Lord in the "latter days" (Deuteronomy 4:30; cf. 31:29 KJV). The prophet Hosea spoke of the future repentance of Israel in the "latter days" (Hosea 3:5 KJV). The prophet Jeremiah predicted numerous events that would occur in the "latter days" (Jeremiah 23:20; 30:24; 48:47; 49:39 KJV). Ezekiel predicted the invasion of Israel by a coalition of nations ("Gog and Magog") in the "latter days" (Ezekiel 38:16 KJV), also using the alternate expression "in the latter years" (Ezekiel 38:8 KJV).

It was against this Old Testament backdrop that our Lord spoke to His disciples about the end of the world. His warnings about false prophets, counterfeit messiahs, natural disasters, and persecution have proven true time and time again throughout the church age.

THE GREAT TRIBULATION

As Jesus looked down the corridor of time to the end of the present age—an age which would be launched by the preaching of the gospel message and by the empowerment of His disciples with the Holy Spirit—He warned of a time of great tribulation ("great distress" [Matthew 24:21]) that would come upon the whole world (Matthew 24:15-28). The "abomination of desolation" (Matthew 24:15 KJV) refers to when Antiochus Epiphanes profaned Jewish temple worship during the intertestamental period (Daniel 9:27; 11:31; 12:11), foreshadowing an even more serious abomination that would occur in the future. Whereas Antiochus offered an unclean pig on the sacred altar of the temple, the Antichrist will offer himself! (2 Thessalonians 2:4).

The act of desecration that Daniel had predicted about Antiochus, a pagan Hellenistic ruler, will be repeated even more seriously in the future. This will signal the beginning of the Great Tribulation on earth. Note that Jesus saw this as a future event, so this abomination is not limited to the past actions of Antiochus. Nor was the abomination fufilled in the Roman destruction of Jerusalem in A.D. 70, since our Lord tied it to the "great tribulation" (KJV) that is "unequaled from the beginning of the world until now—and never to be equaled again" (Matthew 24:21). Our Lord went on to explain that the devastation of the Great Tribulation will be so awful that unless those days were cut short, "no one would survive" (Matthew 24:22).

Jesus further described this coming day of trouble as a time when the sun and moon are darkened and the heavens will be shaken (Matthew 24:29). His description runs parallel to that found in Revelation 16:1-16, where the final hour of the Tribulation is depicted by atmospheric darkness, air pollution, and ecological disaster. These cataclysmic events accompany the return of Christ at the end of the Tribulation.

Christ's return to earth will be marked by "the sign of the Son of Man" appearing in the sky (Matthew 24:30). The nature of this sign is not explained in this passage. Ancient Bible commentators like Chrysostom thought it might be the appearance of a cross in the sky. More recent commentators tend to follow John Peter Lange's view that it is the Shekinah glory of the divine Christ.[4]

Remember our paradigm from the previous chapters: facts, assumptions, speculations.

> **Fact.** Christ will return after the Tribulation, and the sign of the Son of Man will appear in heaven.
> **Assumption.** Christ will return after a seven-year tribulation period and be seen by all the peoples of the earth.
> **Speculation.** 1) The "sign" will be the return of the Bethlehem star; 2) it will be the sign of the cross; 3) the sky will turn blood-red, symbolizing the blood of Christ; and 4) the Shekinah glory of God will gradually unfold into blinding splendor.

Any one of the above speculations could be true. Or, it may be that none of them properly explain what will happen when this "sign" appears. Careful students of prophecy dare not push their speculations as facts. If we observe this simple distinction, we can avoid saying more than the Bible actually says about prophetic events.

ILLUSTRATIONS ABOUT THE LAST DAYS

A dear friend of mine always preached with great intensity; even the supplemental comments in his sermons were screamed. However, after he had preached in a chapel service for one of America's outstanding ministries and screamed the whole time at some of the most committed Christian workers in the world, he was helped greatly when the leader of that organization gave him this simple advice: "Let the truth be obvious and let the illustrations do the shouting."

At this point in the Olivet Discourse, Jesus used several powerful illustrations ("parables") that clearly shouted the truth He was presenting.

1. *Illustration of the Fig Tree* (Matthew 24:32-35)

Jesus used a blossoming fig tree to remind His disciples that they could discern the coming of the end of the age. He said, "Now learn this lesson from the fig tree: As soon as its twigs get tender and its leaves come out, you know that summer is near" (Matthew 24:32). When a tree blooms in the spring, we know that summer is coming. "Even so," Jesus added, "when you see all these things, you know that it [My coming] is near, right at the door" (Matthew 24:33).

The immediate context is illustrative of the point our Lord was making about His coming. Just as God has programmed time indicators into nature (for example, budding trees), so also has He programmed into prophetic history certain time indicators of future events. (Keep in mind that while Scripture sometimes symbolizes Israel as an olive tree, the usage here seems to be that of a general illustration and not a specific prophecy about Israel.)

The generation that lives to "see all these things" come to pass will "not pass away" before Christ returns at the end of the age (Matthew 24:33,34). This difficult saying has been variously interpreted as 1) being fulfilled in the apostles' own lifetime with the destruction of Jerusalem in A.D. 70; 2) referring to the perpetual survival of the race ("generation") of the Jews; 3) the generation of people alive at the time of Christ's return. The Arndt and Gingrich lexicon prefers to translate "generation" (Greek, *genea*) as "age" or "period of time."[5] In other words, the previously listed signs will continue to multiply throughout the church age and reach their ultimate climax at the end of the age—in the generation of those who live to see the entire matter fulfilled.

2. *Illustration of the Flood* (Matthew 24:36-39)

Next our Lord turned to the story of Noah and the great Flood to illustrate the suddenness of His future return. He said, "As it was in the days of Noah, so it will be at the coming of the Son of Man" (Matthew 24:37). He went on to describe the immoral, self-indulgent behavior of Noah's day as typical of the generation who is alive during the last days. They "knew nothing about what would happen" until it was too late (Matthew 24:39).

This illustration, drawn from Genesis 6-9, reminds us that we must always be ready for our Lord to return because "no one knows about that day or hour" (Matthew 24:36). This is one of the most important declarations given in all of biblical prophecy, and yet it is constantly violated. "It says we cannot know the 'day' or the 'hour,' but it doesn't say anything about the year," people will often remark. Others try to argue that Jesus was not ruling out a deeper sense of knowledge by playing off the different Greek words for "know" in the New Testament. The *intent* of the text, however, is clear: No one knows when Christ is coming—so stop trying to guess. Make sure you are prepared *whenever* He comes!

Thus, Jesus admonished, "Keep watch" (Matthew 24:42) and, "Be ready" (Matthew 24:44) for we do not know when He will come. He never told us to calculate any dates or speculate beyond what Scripture predicts. All He said was to "keep watch" (discernment) and "be ready" (determination). These two admonitions are followed by three illustrations that tell us to *keep serving:* The parables of the two servants (Matthew 24:43-51), the ten virgins (Matthew 25:1-13), and the talents of money (Matthew 25:14-30).

3. *Illustrations of the Servants, Virgins, and Money*
    (Matthew 24:43-25:30)
    Jesus clearly stated that the "faithful and wise servant" (Matthew 24:45) was the one found faithfully fulfilling his responsibilities when the master returned. C.S. Lewis put it this way: The best place to be when the inspection comes is at your post. By contrast, the evil servant, says Homer Kent,

"mistakes the uncertainty of the time of coming for a certainty that it will not be soon."[6]

The Parable of the Ten Virgins (Matthew 25:1-13) conveys the same warning to be prepared when the Master comes. These virgins (Greek, *parthenos*) are attendants at the wedding (not the bride), and may symbolize both the saved and unsaved of Israel rather than the church. No matter what their actual identity, the emphasis is still personal preparation and service.

In the Parable of the Talents (Matthew 25:14-30), our Lord again underscored the importance of faithful service in His absence. The "talents" represent monetary values entrusted to us for use in God's service and symbolize the gifts and abilities He has given us with which to serve Him. The "far country" (Matthew 25:14 KJV) seems to be heaven and the master is gone a long time before returning to call his servants to accountability. The fearful servant who hid the money failed to understand the real generosity of the master who wanted him to experience the joys of service.

Note in all three parables the references to "a long time" in Matthew 24:48; 25:5,19. This implies that Jesus (the Master or the Bridegroom) would be gone for a long period of time before He returned. All of these illustrations shout one great truth: Keep serving till Jesus comes again. This message could not be more clear no matter how we interpret the various elements or details of these parables. They remind us that we do not know when our Lord will return; therefore, we must remain faithful to Him until He comes.

The implications of these admonitions, then, are clear:

1. Keep watching.
2. Stay ready.
3. Keep serving.

Perhaps you've read books or heard messages that suggest we should put aside all long-term pursuits because

Christ's return is imminent. But taking such action is dangerous and unrealistic because we have no assurance about when Christ will come. So don't sell all your possessions or give up your job because someone has speculated about the timing of Christ's second coming. If you are in college or graduate school, keep studying—don't drop out! What better goal could Christ find you pursuing than preparing to serve Him in the field of your studies? This is no time to drop out in an act of irresponsible desperation. Hit the books and stay at it.

When I was in college, some students were theorizing that the days were short and the end was near. "Why not drop out now," they said, "and give our lives to serving God?" They missed the point that by studying and preparing for the work world they were serving God, and home they went. That happened quite a few years ago. If they had stayed in school, they would have become better equipped to have an effective ministry for God today.

There are times when God may lead you to take a step of faith in His service, but don't take a step of foolishness. Over the years, I have watched many people give up all responsibility "to serve the Lord," only to watch them take it all back on themselves later. Be faithful in your tasks today, and God will open doors of service tomorrow.

If you have a place of service in your local church, keep at it—don't quit. If you are a teacher, keep teaching. If you are in a choir, keep singing. If you are an elder, keep leading. If you are a deacon, keep serving. And if you are a pastor, keep pastoring. May He find us faithful in that to which He has called us.

JESUS AND THE PROPHETS

In His predictions about the end times, Jesus answered the three questions His disciples asked in Matthew 24:2,3: When will all this happen? What will be the sign of Your coming? And what will be the sign of the end of the age? While the temple was destroyed by the Romans in A.D. 70, we know this wasn't the ultimate fulfillment of His prophetic answers because the preaching of the gospel to the whole world is still in progress today. Thus, both a near judgment of Jerusalem by the Romans and an ultimate judgment by the Antichrist seem to be in view in this passage. LaSor notes: "But regardless of the sequence intended (or that we impose on the passage), Jesus does mention a great tribulation in connection with the end-time events."[7] He further notes that Jesus' reference to the prophet Daniel definitely connects Him to Israel's prophetic heritage.

Daniel's prophecies (Daniel chapter 2 and 7) mention the sequence of four major Gentile world powers that will come in succession: Babylon, Persia, Greece, and Rome. Out of the lattermost kingdom one will rise who will make "war against the saints" (Daniel 7:21). He is also pictured as one who brings "desolation" and "abomination" (Daniel 9:27). This same imagery is used by our Lord in the New Testament. (And in Daniel 11:21-31 we read again of the "contemptible person" who profanes the temple with his armed forces to set up the "abomination that causes desolation.") From the context of Daniel's prophecies, we can conclude that the time of trouble or Great Tribulation involves Daniel's people, the Jews. We can also conclude that the king who will "magnify himself above every god" (Daniel 11:36) is the Antichrist of the last days.

In Jeremiah 30:1-9 the prophet Jeremiah also refers to a "time of trouble for Jacob [Israel]" in the future (verse 7). Jeremiah was writing during the Babylonian Captivity and saw in the distant future an even greater time of trouble.

The book of Revelation pictures the Great Tribulation as Satan's last desperate attempt to destroy the work of God in creation and salvation as well as God's ultimate judgment on the kingdom of Satan through the outpouring of the "wrath of the Lamb" (Revelation 6:16), who is Christ. The Great Tribulation is God's final judgment against the sin and wickedness on earth and results in the resounding declaration, "It is done!" (literally, "It is finished"; Revelation 16:17). Christ's atonement for our sins was finalized with this same declaration on the cross when He lifted up His head and with a loud voice said, "It is finished" (John 19:30; *see also* Matthew 27:50). And at the end of the Great Tribulation, the same cry will go up, "It is finished!"

The final act of God's judgment at the end of the Great Tribulation is generally referred to as the Battle of Armageddon (Revelation 16:16). The other biblical term for this final conflict is the Day of the Lord, which is mentioned several times by the Old Testament prophets.[8] This "day" is viewed by the prophets as a day of darkness and judgment related to the end time.

The prophet Zechariah pictured the Day of the Lord as a time when all the nations will gather together against the city of Jerusalem and the Lord will go forth to defend the city and "on that day his feet will stand on the Mount of Olives, east of Jerusalem, and the Mount of Olives will be split in two from east to west, forming a great valley, with half of the mountain moving north and half moving south" (Zechariah 14:4).

BACK TO THE FUTURE

As we trace the words of Jesus back to the Old Testament prophets, we see that they all point to the future. In a very significant and symbolic gesture, Jesus took His disciples to the Mount of Olives to deliver His most important prophetic message. Not only could they look down on the city of Jerusalem and the temple across the Kidron Valley, but they also were sitting on the very mount from which Jesus would ascend back into heaven (Acts 1:12) and to which He will one day return. He will split it in two when He comes to judge the world and deliver His people (Zechariah 14:4).

The greatest prophetic event of all is yet in the future—the return of Jesus Christ to the Mount of Olives. In His Olivet Discourse our Lord promised to return but set no date, though He implied in His illustrations that He would be gone for a long time (Matthew 24:48; 25:5,19). Yet Jesus also urged His disciples to always be ready for His return. He warned of an imminent and unexpected coming, which tells us we should always be ready.

Jesus also told His disciples that while they were waiting, they were to keep serving Him faithfully. This dual emphasis on serving faithfully and being ready leaves us with a proper balance about matters of biblical prophecy, the return of Christ, and the end of the age. On the one hand, we are to be watching and ready for Him to come at any moment. On the other hand, we are to continue serving Him for as long as He waits. One preacher put it this way: "Live your life as though He could come today, but plan your work as if you had a hundred years."

The most serious announcement in Jesus' message was that *no one* can set any dates for His return (Matthew 24:36). Yet this has been one of the most violated declarations in Scripture. Over the centuries, well-meaning Christians have wanted to assume they were living in the "last days." Something in the human psyche makes us want to believe we are the "terminal generation." Perhaps it is a combination of pride about ourselves and our excitement about the coming of Christ that causes us to read the prophecies of the future through the eyes of the present. But whenever believers have done this, they have jumped from the *facts* of prophecy to their own *assumptions*, and eventually to wild-eyed *speculations*.

Whenever preachers start saying things like, "It will be over in six years," they are speculating and not preaching. How many times have we read over the years that Babylon was being rebuilt or that Israel was planning to rebuild the temple or that the free world was about to collapse?[9] One well-known prophecy preacher who has frequently alluded to dates for the return of Christ "predicted" that the communist flag would fly from Independence Hall in Philadelphia by July 4, 1976. That, of course never happened. This same preacher uses pictures of Mount St. Helens exploding and Israeli license plates with the prefix 666 to tell us again and again that we are out of time. He means well, but does not this kind of blatant speculation eventually cause many people to reject all discussuions about prophecy, including the legitimate ones?

Guessing dates and reading the present era into biblical prophecy is a temptation to which Christians have often succumbed. The end is near, but we dare not claim to know that the end is here. Apocalyptic speculation is a difficult and dangerous enterprise when applied to political and social policies. A person had better be sure he is right before proceeding with his vision for the end.

Chapter 4

⟨ΩⅢ⟩

WHAT'S NEXT ON THE PROPHETIC CALENDAR?

One of the great warnings of prophetic Scripture is that false teaching will bring deception upon professing Christendom in the last days. Jesus Himself warned that "*many* will come in my name, claiming, 'I am the Christ,' and will deceive *many*" (Matthew 24:5, emphasis added). He also predicted that "*many* false prophets will appear and deceive *many* people" (Matthew 24:11, emphasis added). Our Lord said this would continue throughout the church age, but He also spoke of a time at the end of the age in which false messiahs and prophets would perform miracles to deceive the world and even confuse the elect.

The apostle Paul predicted that "there will be terrible times in the last days" and that people will become materialistic, self-centered, abusive, disobedient, ungrateful, unforgiving, and unholy (2 Timothy 3:1-3). Paul then said this same generation would be "lovers of pleasure rather than lovers of God" (2 Timothy 3:4).

Peter prophesied that "in the last days scoffers will come,

scoffing and following their own evil desires" (2 Peter 3:3). These unbelievers will deny the second coming of Christ, saying, "Where is this 'coming' he promised?"(2 Peter 3:4) Jude quoted Peter and added that these men "follow mere natural instincts and do not have the Spirit" (Jude 19).

We should not be surprised, therefore, with the great spiritual confusion that abounds even now: Liberal theologians suggest that there will be no literal return of Christ; Jehovah's Witnesses say He already came secretly in 1914; Mormons tell us they are the only true "Latter-day Saints"; the Unification Church ("Moonies") claim that Sun Myung Moon is the Messiah; *ad infinitum, ad nauseum!*

THE CLOUDS OF SECULARISM

Historian Paul Johnson has called the twentieth century "modern times." [1] Certainly, this century has brought the most incredible technological advances known to the human race: automobiles, airplanes, radios, televisions, computers, and a host of other gadgets that have shaped our lives in ways our forefathers could never have imagined.

Yet with the advancement of modernity has come a restless uneasiness about the spiritual and traditional values of our culture, which are fast slipping away. At times consciously and at other times unconsciously, we seem to be discarding the very ideas that made America great. [2]

Charles Colson opens his book *Against the Night* with this observation: "We sense that things are winding down. . . . Our great civilization may not yet lie in smoldering ruins, but the enemy is within the gates. The times seem to smell of sunset." [3]

Throughout the twentieth century, secularism encroached upon and replaced the Judeo-Christian values of our society. God was gradually and systematically removed from any place of prominence in our culture and our intellectual lives. Scientism turned science into a religion which taught that natural laws, not spiritual principles, guide the universe. The entrenchment of the theory of evolution in our schools made God irrelevant to our culture. Men now see themselves as little more than glorified animals whose highest instinct is self-gratification.

We should not be surprised, then, when educators, sociologists, psychologists, and other assessors of life tell us that ours is a self-centered culture.[4] The self-indulgent pursuit of money, power, and fame has plunged our whole society down the toboggan slide of narcissism.

Have We Lost Our Minds?

Joining hands with secularism is the philosophical concept of *relativism,* which teaches that there is no absolute truth. Something is viewed as being true only because a group of people accept it as true. Relativism dethrones all absolutes, including God and His laws. The great danger of this worldview is that it leads to a naive acceptance of secularism. Nothing is seen as right or wrong in itself, but only as it relates to its context.

The influence of relativism has affected nearly every area of our culture. One of the most thought-provoking books to appear in the 1980s was Allan Bloom's *The Closing of the American Mind,* which explored the intellectual vacuum of our time.[5] Bloom argues that today's students are unlike any generation that has preceded them because they have been robbed of truth and dignity by the philosophy of relativism, which permeates higher education.

"Today's students are no longer interested in noble causes," Bloom bemoans. "There is an indifference to such things for relativism has extinguished the real motive of education."[6] He observes that today's students have generally abandoned themselves to the pursuit of the good life or what Arthur Levine called "going first-class on the Titanic."[7]

The greatest danger of relativism is that it leads to the appeasement of evil. If all truth is relative, then all ethics are situational. If I have part of the truth and you have part of the truth, then neither of us has the whole truth. Once we accept this concept, we have no basis on which to judge any action as morally right or wrong.

The unborn, the elderly, the retarded, and the handicapped are also expendable in the relativist worldview. Consequently, we should not be surprised that our society, which embraces relativism, is willing to tolerate abortion, euthanasia, and even infanticide. And it will not take long for that same perspective to be used to suggest the elimination of people who oppose what is best for the advancement of the new world order.

Former Surgeon General C. Everett Koop called this indifference to the sanctity of life "the slide to Auschwitz." It is the same intellectual journey that led to Hitler's Nazi atrocities under the guise of helping the evolutionary process of natural selection eliminate undesirable life forms.

New Age Mysticism

Relativism also opens the door to mysticism. Modern man has reached a point where he doesn't really want to face the logical consequences of a secular world without God, so he is turning to a kind of scientific mysticism popularized as the New Age movement.[8]

New Age thinking is a do-it-yourself religion with a smorgasbord of options: spiritism, witchcraft, channeling, transcendentalism, Oriental mysticism, and transpersonal psychology. Intellectually, it grows out of the belief that the world is now evolving spiritually, producing a great "planetary consciousness" that will eventually lead to a new world order.

New Agers are calling for the total transformation of society along social and political lines—a transformantion consistent with their own beliefs. They see mankind emerging into human consciousness and potential by declaring its own deification, leaving God "watching from a distance," as the top song of 1990 put it ("From a Distance," sung by Bette Middler).

The Great Brain Robbery

It has been nearly 30 years since Francis Schaeffer argued that the rationalism of our secular society would eventually rob our culture of its rationality.[9] He was right! We are now reaping the consequences of a world gone mad intellectually. Feelings have replaced truth as the benchmark of our culture. "If it feels good, do it" was a slogan in the 1970s, but it is the reality of everyday life in the 1990s.

As we rapidly approach the end of the century and the dawn of the third millennium of church history, it is clear that the mindset of our society is shifting dramatically. While we cannot predict that current intellectual trends will necessarily lead to the deception of the last days (of which Scripture warns), it would certainly seem that the trends are not in our favor. Undoubtedly, the deck is stacked against us in the battle for the minds of men.

The intellectual bankruptcy of our culture is indeed the great brain robbery of our times. Eastern Europe, the Soviet Union, and even parts of the Arab world are opening up to Western culture, but what do we have to offer them other than the material goods of our indulgent society? Most of what we send them overseas only trap foreigners in the same mindless pursuit of self-indulgence in which we ourselves are caught.

Whether the final deception of the end times stems directly from the intellectual developments of our own age remains to be seen. What *is* clear, however, is that the Christian consensus that once dominated Western culture is now shattered and is unlikely to be recovered. We are already mired in the quicksands of secularism, relativism, and mysticism.

The Hope of the Church

The hope of the church is the return of Jesus Christ. She does not await the last days in the same sense that the rest of the world does. Rene Pache said, "The signs of the times warn her that her deliverance is near; the sufferings here below, the last assaults of the enemy, cause her to say ever more ardently, 'Lord Jesus, come quickly!' "[10]

The church awaits a Person, not destruction. Peter explained that the present world is "reserved for fire, being kept for the day of judgment and destruction of *ungodly* men" (2 Peter 3:7, emphasis added). While it's true that the church is told to prepare for suffering and persecution throughout the church age, she is *not* pictured in Scripture as the object of God's final wrath. In fact, our Lord said to the church, "I will also keep you from the hour of trial that is going to come upon the whole world" (Revelation 3:10). Notice, the church is to be kept *from* (literally, "out of"), not *through*, the hour of trouble that is coming.

What Is the Rapture?

The rapture (or translation) of the church is often paralleled to the "raptures" of Enoch (Genesis 5:24) and Elijah (2 Kings 2:11-12) or the ascension of Christ (Acts 1:9), all of whom were "taken up" into heaven. The Bible clearly states, "The Lord Himself will come down from heaven, with a loud command, with the voice of the archangel and with the trumpet call of God, and the dead in Christ will rise first. After that, we who are still alive and are left will be *caught up* together with them in the clouds to meet the Lord in the air. And so we will be with the Lord forever" (1 Thessalonians 4:16-17, emphasis added).

In the rapture, both those who have died in Christ over the centuries and those who are alive when He returns will be taken up. This is the event our Lord spoke of when He said, "A time is coming when all who are in their graves will hear his voice and come out" (John 5:28). Believers are pictured as being raised to *life* (the first resurrection) and unbelievers as being raised to *judgment* (the second resurrection). In reference to Christians, the Bible says, "They came to life and reigned with Christ a thousand years. . . . This is the first resurrection" (Revelation 20:4-5). We also read about the second resurrection, comprised of unbelievers: "The rest of the dead did not come to life until the thousand years were ended" (Revelation 20:5).

When Will the Rapture Occur?

The *fact* that there will be a rapture is clearly taught in Scripture. The real debate is over *when* it will occur. *Pre-Tribulationists* believe the church will be raised before the tribulation period.[11] *Mid-Tribulationists* believe the church will enter the Tribulation and be raptured at some midpoint during it.[12] *Post-Tribulationists* believe the church will go through the Tribulation as the suffering "saints" in the book of Revelation. They view the rapture as coming at the end of the Tribulation.[13]

Let me suggest several reasons why I believe the rapture will occur before the Tribulation.

1. *Christ promised to keep the church from the Tribulation.* In Revelation 3:10, the risen Christ said the church would be *kept from* (literally, "preserved" or "protected *out* of") the hour of trial that is coming on the whole world. This is no local judgment or persecution, but rather a worldwide judgment of God. The events described in the Apocalypse are acts of divine retribution. They are not merely human persecutions.

2. *The judgments of the tribulation period are called "the wrath of the Lamb."* Revelation 6:16 depicts the cataclysmic judgments of the end times as the wrath of Christ, the Lamb of God. Note that later in the book of Revelation the church is portrayed as the bride of the Lamb (Revelation 19:7-9). Clearly, she is not the object of His wrath against unbelievers. Nor is it likely He will condemn the church, which He is going to marry, with the rest of the world. He may purge her to cleanse her, but He will not judge her for unbelief.

3. *Jesus told His disciples to pray that they would escape the Tribulation.* In Luke 21:36 Jesus said, "Be always on the watch, and pray that you may be able to escape all

IS THE WORD *RAPTURE* IN THE BIBLE?

⚬⚬⚬ ⚬⚬⚬ ⚬⚬⚬

The word *rapture* is from the word *rapere*, found in the expression "caught up" in the Latin translation of 1 Thessalonians 4:17. However, the rapture could be scripturally referred to as the *harpazo*, which is the Greek word translated "caught up" in 1 Thessalonians 4:17. This same phrase is found in Acts 8:39, where Philip was caught away by the Holy Spirit, and in 2 Corinthians 12:2,4, when Paul was caught up into the third heaven.

The rapture could be known as the *allasso*, from the Greek word translated "changed" in 1 Corinthians 15:51-52. *Allasso* is used also to describe the final renewal and transformation of the heavens and the earth (*see* Hebrews 1:12).

While the English word rapture is not used in the King James Version of the Bible, the concept of the rapture is clearly taught in God's Word. The Church will be "caught up" (Greek, *harpazo*) in the clouds to meet the Lord in the air. Having been "caught up," we shall be "gathered together" (Greek, *episunagoges* [cf. 2 Thessalonians 2:1] in the clouds. The raptured church is pictured as the great "assembly" (synagogue) in the sky. Thus, the church will be "caught up" and "gathered together" with her Lord.

The concept of the rapture is clearly taught in the New Testament. So much so, that every system of eschatology must make room for it—even those systems that reject the pretribulational rapture view. If Christ is coming for His bride to take her home to heaven, the rapture is inevitable.

---

* Taken from: Harold L. Willmington, *The King Is Coming*, Wheaton: IL Tyndale House, 1991, p. 7. Used with permission.

that is about to happen, and that you may be able to stand before the Son of Man." Remember, even Lot was given a chance to escape Sodom before divine judgment fell (Genesis 19; cf. Luke 17:28-36).

4. *Jesus' coming in the clouds means the church's deliverance has come.* Jesus told His disciples that when He comes in the clouds, "stand up and lift up your heads, because your redemption is drawing near" (Luke 21:28). The hope for the church is not surviving the Tribulation but escaping it.

5. *God will call His ambassadors home before declaring war on the world.* In 2 Corinthians 5:20, believers are called "Christ's ambassadors" who appeal to the world to be reconciled to God. God will recall His ambassadors at the rapture before He unleashes His final judgments on the unbelieving world.

6. *Moral restraint will disappear when the church is taken.* Paul's words in 2 Thessalonians 2:1-11 refer to the "coming of our Lord" and "our being gathered to him" (verse 1). These verses also warn that the "man of lawlessness" (the Antichrist, verse 3) will be revealed only *after* the restraining power of God is removed from the world. While some people assume this restraining influence is the Holy Spirit who indwells the church, it seems more likely that the restrainer is the church itself, which is removed before the Tribulation. Her "salt and light" ministry of restraining evil in the world will have been completed, whereas the omnipresent Holy Spirit will continue His ministry on through the tribulation period, during which time a host of Jews and Gentiles will be converted to faith in Christ (Revelation 7:9-14).

7. *The rapture will happen in the twinkling of an eye.* The Bible says, "We will not all sleep [in death], but we will all be changed—in a flash, in the twinkling of an eye, at the last trumpet. For the trumpet will sound, the dead will be raised imperishable, and we [those living at the rapture] will be changed" (1 Corinthians 15:51-52). This instantaneous disappearance will conclude the church's earthly ministry.

8. *The rapture will take place in the air.* The Bible states that we who are alive on earth at the time of the rapture will be "caught up . . . to meet the Lord in the air" (1 Thessalonians 4:17). This is very much in contrast to our Lord's coming *with* His saints when He returns to the earth after the Tribulation. At that time He will split the Mount of Olives. The prophet Zechariah said, "Then the LORD my God will come, and all the holy ones with him" (Zechariah 14:5). At the rapture we go *up* and at the return we come back *down* with Christ.

9. *The woman who suffers persecution during the Tribulation symbolizes Israel.* The woman, Israel, delivers the male child, or Christ (Revelation 12:1-2,5-6). Israel as a nation brought forth Christ; He then established the church. Since He is its founder and not its descendant, the woman cannot be the church. This symbolism clearly indicates that Israel, not the church, will suffer. The church is absent, already having been raptured.

10. *The marriage of Christ (the Lamb) and His bride (the church) takes place before the Battle of Armageddon.* The Scripture describes the fall of the Antichrist's kingdom (symbolically called "Babylon") in Revelation chapters 17-18. But, before Christ returns from heaven on a white horse to conquer the Beast and the False

Contrast Between
the Rapture and the Return

Rapture

1. Christ comes *for* His own
   (John 14:3; 1 Thessalonians
   14:17; 2 Thessalonians 2:1).
2. He comes in the air
   (1 Thessalonians 4:17).
3. He *claims* His bride
   (1 Thessalonians 4:17).
4. Removal of *believers*
   (1 Thessalonians 4:17).
5. *Only* His own see Him
   (1 Thessalonians 4:13-18).
6. *Tribulation* begins
   (2 Thessalonians 1:6-9).
7. Saved are *delivered from
   wrath* (1 Thessalonians
   1:10; 5–9).
8. *No signs* precede rapture
   (1 Thessalonians 5:1-3).
9. Focus: *Lord and church*
   (1 Thessalonains 4:13-18).
10. *World* is deceived
    (2 Thessalonians 2:3-12).

Return

1. Christ *comes with* His own
   (1 Thessalonians 3:13. Jude 14;
   Revelation 19:14).
2. He comes to the *earth*
   (Zechariah 14:4; Acts 1:11).
3. He comes *with* His bride
   (Revelation 19:6-14).
4. Manifestation of *Christ*
   (Malachi 4:2).
5. *Every eye* shall see Him
   (Revelation 1:7).
6. Millennial *kingdom* begins
   (Revelation 20:1-7).
7. Unsaved *experience the wrath*
   of God (Revelation 6:12-17).
8. *Signs* precede second coming
   (Luke 21:11,15).
9. Focus: *Israel and kingdom*
   (Matthew 24:14).
10. *Satan* is bound
    (Revelation 20:1-2).

Taken from E. Hindson, "The Rapture and the Return," in *When the Trumpet Sounds* (Eugene, OR: Harvest House, 1995), pp. 157-58.

WRATH OF THE LAMB INVOKED
(Revelation 5-19)

⚍⚍⚍ ⚍⚍⚍ ⚍⚍⚍

1. He pours out the seven seal judgments (6:1-17; 8:1-9:21)
2. He allows the devil to reign (12-13)
3. He pours out the seven vial judgments (14-16)
4. He destroys the world's religious systems (17)
5. He destroys the world's political and economic systems (18)
6. He defeats sinners and Satan at Armageddon (19; 1-19,21)
7. He condemns the Antichrist and False Prophet into hell (19:20)

FIRST DIVINE PUNISHMENT
The Lamb Pours Out the Seven Seal Judgments
Revelation 6:1-17; 8:1-9:21 See also Matthew 24:4-8

1st seal	White Horse	Cold War (6:2)
2nd seal	Red Horse	Hot war (6:3-4)
3rd seal	Black Horse	Famine (6:5-6)
4th seal	Pale Horse	Widespread death by way, starvation and wild beasts (6:7-8)
5th seal	The cry of the martyred (6:9-11)	
6th seal	Earth's greatest earthquake, earth's greatest cosmic disturbance, earth's greatest prayer meeting (6:12-17)	

INTERLUDE
A short period between the sixth and seventh seals (7:1-17)
The conversion and call of the 144,000 (7:1-18)
The conversion and call of a great multitude (7:9-17)

7TH SEAL
Composed of Seven Trumpets (8:1-11:19)

First trumpet (8:7) — One-third of vegetation destroyed
Second trumpet (8:8-9) — One-third of ocean life and ships destroyed
Third trumpet (8:10-11) — One-third of fresh water poisoned
Fourth trumpet (8:12) — One-third of sun, moon, and starts darkened
Fifth trumpet (9:1-12) — their location (9:1) their leaders (9:1,11) their torment (9:3-4) their duration (9:5-6) their description (9:7-10)
First Hellish Invasion of Demons upon this Earth
Sixth trumpet (9:13-21) — leaders (9:14) source (9:14) number (9:16) duration (9:15,18) damage (9:15,18) description (9:17-19) results (9:20-21)
Second Hellish Invasion of Demons upon this Earth

INTERLUDE
(10:1-11:14)
The Message of the Angel of God (10:1-11)
The Measuring of the Temple of God (11:1-2)
The Ministry of the Witnesses of God (11:3-14)

Seventh Trumpet (11:15-19) The King Is Coming

Prophet (Revelation 19:11-21), we read that "the wedding of the Lamb has come, and his bride has made herself ready" (Revelation 19:7-8). This clearly indicates the bride will go to heaven first and then she will return with Christ in the host of the "armies of heaven . . . riding on white horses and dressed in fine linen, white and clean" (Revelation 19:14).

THE COMING DAY OF WRATH

The Old Testament prophets called it the "day of the LORD" (Joel 1:15) or the "day of vengeance of our God" (Isaiah 61:2). They described it as a day of darkness (Amos 5:18) and of fire (Zephaniah 1:18) burning as hot as a furnace (Malachi 4:1). "That day will be a day of wrath, a day of distress and anguish, a day of trouble and ruin, a day of darkness and gloom. . . . because they have sinned against the LORD" (Zephaniah 1:15-17). This day of divine judgment against unbelievers will consume the whole world (Zephaniah 1:18).

The Old Testament closes with a warning about the coming day of the Lord (Malachi 4). Yet this final chapter also promises hope for those who revere His name. These people will "go out and leap" for joy. Malachi also prophesied that before that "great and dreadful day," the prophet Elijah would return (verse 5). Jesus said this promise was fulfilled in the coming of John the Baptist (Matthew 11:14).

The Great Tribulation is the period of divine judgment that immediately precedes the coming of Christ in power and great glory. The prophet Ezekiel called it "the day of the LORD . . . a day of clouds, a time of doom for the nations [Gentiles]" (Ezekiel 30:3). He even named many of those nations: Egypt, Cush, Put, Lydia, Arabia, and Libya (Ezekiel 30:5).

In recent years it has been customary for pre-Tribulationists to see two great battles coming in the future:

- Magog and her Arab allies against Israel
- Antichrist and his kingdom against Israel

Older pre-Tribulationists, like Rene Pache, believe there is only one great end-time battle, noting that many of the same nations are named as falling on the "day of the Lord" (Armageddon) in Ezekiel 30:1-8. No matter how a person interprets these end-time conflicts, the Bible clearly teaches that Israel, not the church, is the target of these attacks and that in the final battle Christ will return with His church saints, His bride, to deliver Israel and complete the unity of God's people.

The final battle of Armageddon is called the . . .

- wrath of the Lord (Isaiah 26:20)
- hot anger of the Lord (Ezekiel 38:18)
- dread of the Lord (Isaiah 2:10)
- vengeance of God (Isaiah 35:4)
- harvest of judgment (Micah 4:11-12; Revelation 14:14-20)
- grapes of wrath (Isaiah 63:1-6; Revelation 19:15)
- great banquet of God (Ezekiel 39:17-20; Revelation 19:17-18)

The devastation of Armageddon will be so extensive that it is probably best viewed as a *war* that destroys most of the earth as well as a final *battle* focused in the Middle East. This also best explains the development of catastrophic events in Revelation chapters 15–19.

The carnage will be so great that most of the earth's population will be annihilated. The plant life all over the planet will be nearly destroyed. The air and water will be severely polluted. "Babylon" will be burned up. The armies of the Antichrist will be wiped out, and the Beast and the False Prophet will be thrown into the lake of fire (Revelation 19:20).

The final devastation will be the self-destructive acts of a world gone mad without God. The Bible says:

- darkness will reign (Isaiah 5:30; Zechariah 14:7)
- the heavens shall be shaken (Isaiah 34:4)

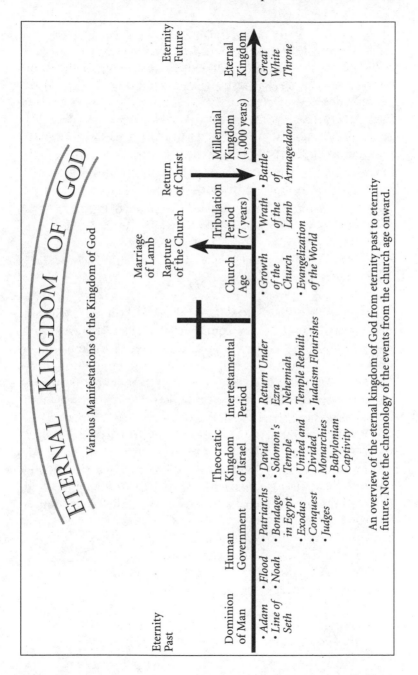

ETERNAL KINGDOM OF GOD

Various Manifestations of the Kingdom of God

Eternity Past	Dominion of Man	Human Government	Theocratic Kingdom of Israel	Intertestamental Period	Church Age	Tribulation Period (7 years)	Return of Christ	Millennial Kingdom (1,000 years)	Eternal Kingdom	Eternity Future

Dominion of Man
• Adam
• Line of Seth

Human Government
• Flood
• Noah

Theocratic Kingdom of Israel
• Patriarchs
• Bondage in Egypt
• Exodus
• Conquest
• Judges
• David
• Solomon's Temple
• United and Divided Monarchies
• Babylonian Captivity

Intertestamental Period
• Return Under Ezra
• Nehemiah
• Temple Rebuilt
• Judaism Flourishes

Church Age
• Growth of the Church
• Evangelization of the World

Marriage of Lamb
Rapture of the Church

Tribulation Period (7 years)
• Wrath of the Lamb

Return of Christ
• Battle of Armageddon

Eternal Kingdom
• Great White Throne

An overview of the eternal kingdom of God from eternity past to eternity future. Note the chronology of the events from the church age onward.

- the earth will quake (Isaiah 29:6; Zechariah 14:4-5)
- huge hailstones will fall from heaven (Revelation 16:21)
- the invading host will destroy itself (Zechariah 14:13)

The prophet Zechariah describes this day in vivid terms:

> The LORD will strike all the nations that fought against Jerusalem: Their flesh will rot while they are standing on their feet, their eyes will rot in their sockets, and their tongues will rot in their mouths. On that day men will be stricken by the LORD with great panic. Each man will seize the hand of another, and they will attack each other (Zechariah 14:12-13).

CHRIST'S KINGDOM ON EARTH

As terrible as the Battle of Armageddon will be, it will not mark the end of the earth. Zechariah 14:16 tells us that the "survivors from all the nations that have attacked Jerusalem will go up year after year to worship the King, the LORD Almighty." Revelation 20:1-6 tells us that Satan will be bound 1,000 years while we serve as "priests of God and of Christ" (verse 6) and reign with Jesus during those 1,000 years.

Premillennialists, in general, interpret this as a time when resurrected and raptured saints rule with Christ over the survivors of the Great Tribulation, who live on earth during Christ's 1,000-year earthly rule. This is generally considered to be a time of peace and prosperity unparalleled in human history.

Chapter 5

⚬⚬⚬

The Coming Darkness

The spiritual vacuum of our times is being filled with the darkness of evil. We are no longer a predominantly Christian society. The symbols and trappings of Christianity remain, but the heart and soul of it have been polluted by the secular pursuit of life without God. More and more it is evident that the majority of people in today's world are looking in all the wrong places to find meaning and purpose for their lives.

Aleksandr Solzhenitsyn has remarked, "The forces of Evil have begun their decisive offensive."[1] So it seems that we are digging in for what may well be the final onslaught against biblical Christianity. The final blow may not come from a direct offensive of anti-Christian sentiment, but rather from sheer neglect of its message. After all, what better way to undermine the gospel than to live as though it did not exist?

We see the evidence of that neglect in every form of art, music, literature, and film. Those depicted are void of spiritual values, conflicts, and concerns. People are so totally ignorant of biblical truth that they go about their lives as if there were no

God. Movies are full of characters like the one portrayed by Michael Douglas in *Wall Street,* who bellows out: "Greed is good! Greed works!" Then there is the proverbial prostitute characterized by Julia Roberts in *Pretty Woman,* who defends her profession with the profound remark, "You gotta make a living."

These are just a few of the many examples of non-Christian or even anti-Christian sentiment that permeate modern culture. Although there are many genuine believers who have not capitulated to secularism, materialism, and pragmatism, still these attitudes can be found even within the Christian community. It is as though the darkness is so great that even we who are believers can't always find our way through the maze of modern life.

We abound in conveniences that make our lives easier. Jet airplanes speed us across the country and around the world in a matter of hours. Satellite transmitters bring world events to our televisions within seconds. Air conditioning cools us in the summer, and central heating warms us in the winter. Life is no longer a struggle for survival. It is often the pursuit of life, liberty, and happiness just as our forefathers planned.

But the freedom to pursue life often allows us to become sidetracked from its true meaning and purpose. Most people are so busy these days that they can't sit still long enough to enjoy the life they have. Most of us overextend ourselves to the point that even our leisure time often becomes a hassle.

THE NEW DARK AGES

Charles Colson has noted that centuries ago, the church had to stand alone against the barbarian culture of the Dark Ages.[2] Classical Rome had become corrupt from within and fell to successive waves of warring bands of illiterate barbarian tribes. While Medieval Europe lay in the shambles of spiritual darkness, the church took a stand and fought illiteracy, moral degradation, and political corruption. The barbarians could not withstand the stubborn resistance of Christian civilization. In time, Europe emerged from the Dark Ages into an era of spiritual and intellectual creativity and growth.

Colson sees the church at a similar crisis point today—confronting the New Dark Ages. The Bible predicts that a time of spiritual apostasy ("falling away") will precede the revealing of the Antichrist ("man of sin").[3] The book of Revelation describes this apostasy as the religion of the "great whore" (17:1 KJV). She is the epitome of false religion and spiritual adultery. By contrast, the New Testament church is pictured as a virgin betrothed to Christ.

Most evangelicals believe this apostasy is made up of people who outwardly profess Christianity but do not possess the Spirit of God in their hearts. Peter Lalonde argues that the apostate whore is not made up of any particular denomination, but of "all those who do not truly love the Lord."[4] Many people view the false religion of the last days as a combination of corrupted Catholicism, liberal Protestantism, and New Age mysticism all rolled into one grand deception.

The Spirit of Antichrist

There is no doubt in my mind that the stage is already set for the final rise of apostasy. The apostle John warned centuries ago that the "spirit of the antichrist" is already at work through the lust of the flesh, the lust of the eyes, and the pride of life (1 John 2:16-19; 4:1-4). He added that there are "many antichrists" who "went out from us" because they "did not really belong to us" (1 John 2:18-19).

In Scripture, people who profess Christ but do not know Him and do not possess His Spirit are called little antichrists because they express the spirit and attitude of the Antichrist. But they only prefigure the Antichrist, who is described in the Bible as the "man of sin," the "son of perdition," and the "beast . . . out of the sea."

The identity of the Antichrist is not fully disclosed in

Scripture. Therefore it is a waste of time to speculate about his identity. Only after the church is taken out of the world will the "mystery of iniquity," which is already at work, be fully released and then shall the "wicked one" be revealed (*see* 2 Thessalonians 2:7-8 KJV).

The possiblity that such a great deceiver could come upon the world scene instantly and dramatically may seem remote to some. But many New Agers are already proposing such a scenario in the future. Barbara Marx Hubbard, executive director of the World Future society and a Democratic party nominee for Vice President of the United States in 1984, believes that a mass transformation could trigger a "Planetary Pentecost" that would empower millions of people at once in a quantum leap toward world wholeness.[5] Hubbard sees this as "the great instant of cooperation" that will be triggered by some great cosmic event.

Many evangelical Christians believe the rapture of the church will be just such an event! It will have global significance and will most likely frighten the entire world population. Thus, it will have to be "explained" in some manner. The Bible warns that the explanation which is given will be a lie that brings "powerful delusion" to the whole unbelieving world (*see* 2 Thessalonians 2:11). Only time will tell whether New Age "prophecies" are setting the stage for this deception. But the mindset of New Age thinking certainly comes dangerously closer to this than anything we have seen yet in this century.

LEFT BEHIND

While the anticipation of Christ's coming to rapture the church is the blessed hope of the believer, it is a sobering matter for the people who are left behind. They are described as deceived unbelievers who have no hope. They will succumb to the great lie and will perish and be condemned (2 Thessalonians 2:10-12). This is not a pretty picture, but it is God's warning to a defiant and unbelieving world.

When the Antichrist rises to power, he will oppose God, exalt himself above God, and even claim to be God (2 Thessalonians 2:3-4). The Bible warns us that the Antichrist will be empowered by Satan himself to do miraculous signs and wonders (2 Thessalonians 2:9). He will be assisted by the False Prophet (Revelation 19:20), who encourages the worship of the Antichrist as God.

Bible prophecy tells us that the Antichrist's reign will comprise a one-world system. He will be empowered by Satan to deceive the world and control the world's economy. No one will be able to buy or sell except those who have "the mark, which is the name of the beast or the number of his name" (Revelation 13:17). The people who are left behind at the rapture will not be able to escape this global system set up during the Tribulation.

Those who are left behind at the rapture will witness the rise of the Antichrist, his false promise of peace, his persecution of believers, and his eventual war with God, which will culminate at Armageddon. Some of these people will come to faith in Christ during this time, but they will be martyred and executed for their belief.

THE GREAT DECEPTION

Many of the people who are left behind will be deceived and never come to true faith in Christ. They will be trapped in the global empire ruled by the satanic forces of the Antichrist and the False Prophet. Peter Lalonde observes:

> Regardless of the way the Antichrist rises to power, and regardless of the exact nature of the signs and wonders that accompany his rise, we know that he will accomplish three main objectives. First, he will convince the Jews that he is their long-awaited Messiah. Secondly, he will convince the false church that is left behind after the rapture that he is the true Christ. Finally, he will convince everyone that

> this is actually the beginning of the millennial
> period . . . during which people live together in
> peace and harmony for a thousand years.[6]

Jesus Himself warned against false Christs, false prophets, deceptive miracles, and a counterfeit messiah. He said: "Watch out that no one deceives you. For many will come in my name, claiming, 'I am the Christ,' and will deceive many" (Matthew 24:4-5). This warning came at the beginning of Christ's own prophecy about the end times, the Olivet Discourse (Matthew 24–25).

We can only guess how and when this deception will occur. But even the most skeptical person must admit that our world's concepts of truth and reality have changed drastically in the past 50 years. People are no longer concerned about what is true; rather, they want to know what works for them.

The powerful and revealing book *The Agony of Deceit,* edited by Michael Horton, provides vivid details of the erroneous and even heretical ideas being promoted by some extremist television preachers.[7] The tragedy of our times is that even well-intended believers are often caught up in doctrinal error and deceit and don't even know it. Every human being is vulnerable to error, and when the ultimate deception comes, no one will be able to withstand it.

WHOSE FAULT IS IT?

The Roman orator Cicero once said, "It is impossible to know the truth and not be held responsible." Yet today we find millions of Americans who realize something has gone wrong in our country but who also have not taken the initiative to find out what it is or what to do about it. Too many Americans blame politicians for the sad state of affairs we are in today. But it is we, the American people, who have allowed these conditions to come about.

Over a decade ago, Marvin Stone observed the growing trend of callousness in our society. He said, "We shrug off almost everything now, moving on to the next fleeting titilla-tion. It's as if we are beyond making distinctions, beyond car-ing ... after two centuries we have reached a consensus of indifference."[8]

The real tragedy of our times is that many people are neglecting the spiritual values that made our country great and instead are pursuing the temporal and material values that can never bring lasting satisfaction to the human soul. People are spending their lives and money lusting after things that can never satisfy their deepest needs.

IS THERE ANY HOPE?

Sin is the transgression of God's law. When a man does what is right in his own eyes, he is really saying that it does not matter to him what God thinks about it. The Bible reminds us: "Righteousness exalts a nation, but sin is a disgrace to any people" (Proverbs 14:34). People or nations cannot ignore God's laws, live as they please, and expect to be happy and blessed. The refusal to listen to God is a sure path to judgment. However, don't get the impression that God delights in meting out His judgment, because He does not. God's heart breaks when He sees sin in our lives, and His punishments are meant to correct us and bring us to repentance.

God gave Israel a wonderful promise: "If my people, who are called by my name, will humble themselves and pray and seek my face and turn from their wicked ways, then will I hear from heaven and will forgive their sin and will heal their land" (2 Chronicles 7:14). As Christians, we too must repent of our sins believing that He will forgive our sins and heal our land as well. While this promise was given initially to God's covenant people Israel, it is not inappropriate to apply it to God's people today.

God's people are the only ones who can make a lasting dif-ference in this world. And that is only by the grace of God. As the Lord directs and guides us, we can be the light of the world in a time of spiritual darkness.

The Only Answer

Ours has often been characterized as an empty and meaningless generation. The mindless pursuit of personal pleasure and the abandonment of God's moral laws have left millions of people empty and desperately seeking real satisfaction in their lives. Tragically, the basic human needs for love, acceptance, companionship, intimacy, and personal affirmation are totally lost in the pursuit of self-gratification—a pursuit that leaves God out of the picture. Only God can fill the spiritual vacuum of the human soul. He and He alone can give us the love and acceptance we really need.

Though we have more conveniences, more technology, and more leisure time than any previous generation, most people today are not happy. When will they learn that only God can satisfy the longings of the human heart? Jesus said, "I have come that they may have life, and have it to the full ['more abundantly']"(John 10:10 KJV).

Our generation must face the fact that they will never find happiness without God. As long as people continue seeking for the meaning and purpose of life without God, they will never find it. Only when men and women come to the end of themselves and turn to God will they find the true meaning of life.

Chapter 6

❦

THE GATHERING STORM

Darkness was already falling in Chicago at 3:36 P.M. on December 2, 1942, when a group of scientists huddled together on the dimly lit squash court of The University of Chicago's abandoned football stadium. Following a technique used in 1939 by German scientists who had succeeded in splitting the atom, they produced the first controlled nuclear fission chain reaction in history. Less than three years later, their discovery would lead to the most dreadful weapon in human history—the atomic bomb.

In a stretch of desert 50 miles from Alamogordo, New Mexico, the first atomic bomb was exploded at 5:20 A.M. on July 16, 1945. Then, less than three weeks later, President Harry Truman gave the orders to drop an atomic bomb on Hiroshima, Japan, at 8:15 A.M. on August 6. It leveled two-thirds of the city of 350,000 people in the most incredible decimation in human history.

By 1949 the Soviet Union had also developed the atomic bomb, and the Cold War was under way. Then, on November 1,

1952, the United States tested the first hydrogen bomb on a small atoll in the Pacific Ocean. The explosion was so devastating that it blew the one-mile-long island of Elugelab right out of the Pacific, leaving a 175-foot-deep hole in its place in the ocean floor! A frightening new era of apocalyptic proportions had dawned.

LIVING WITH THE BOMB

Despite all the miscalculations of the past, many people believe that the storm clouds are gathering on the horizon of humanity today. Ours is a very different world from any that has ever preceded it. On February 7, 1991, Army General Colin Powell, at that time the Chairman of the Joint Chiefs of Staff for the United States Armed Forces, warned: "The Soviet Union still remains the one country in the world that could destroy us in thirty minutes!"[1] We live in a day when it is possible to destroy the entire world with nuclear weapons in one hour.

While the desire for peace clings to the deepest crevice of the human heart, ultimately, the prospects for global destruction are greater than they are for global peace. Undoubtedly, the present crises in our world will result in some attempted settlement and peaceful solution. But beyond the coming peace is the final holocaust.

Sir Winston Churchill said that in the twentieth century "war began to enter into its kingdom as the potential destroyer of the human race." Today the vast coalition of nations and the modern weapons of warfare are such that the enterprise of slaughter can be, as Churchill put it, "executed on a scale and with a perseverance never before imagined."[2]

THE NUCLEAR AGE MENTALITY

Since 1945, when the atomic bomb was dropped on Hiroshima, Japan, mankind has lived with the threat of nuclear annihilation. The "baby boomers," those born in the population boom after World War II, could just as easily be called the generation of the bomb. Many psychologists believe that people in this generation do not think like previous generations because they have to live with the reality of their own vulnerability every day.

Educator Arthur Levine has described the current mentality as "going first class on the Titanic!"[3] In his study sponsored by the Carnegie Foundation for the Advancement of Teaching, Levine found that today's students are self-centered, individualistic "escapists" who want little responsibility for solving society's problems, but who also want society to provide them with the opportunity to fulfill their pleasures. They have given up noble causes because they have given up any real hope of solving the world's problems. They see themselves on a hopeless voyage destined to disaster. Unable to turn the ship around, they simply clamor for the first-class seats so they can enjoy the ride until the inevitable strikes.

It should not surprise us, therefore, that people today will spare almost no expense for "living the good life." They are trying to pretend everything is all right even though they know it isn't.

THE PROLIFERATION OF NUCLEAR WEAPONS

The Center for Defense Information estimates that the United States alone has an arsenal of over 35,000 nuclear weapons and is capable of producing them at the rate of three per day. Each of these bombs carries the equivalent of 460 million tons of TNT—35,000 times *greater* than the power of the atomic bomb that killed 70,000 people in Hiroshima in 1945.

The Soviet Union's 100-megaton H-bombs are each capable of creating an all-consuming firestorm 170 miles in diameter. Just 20 of these superbombs could destroy 75 percent of the population of the United States in less than 1 hour! American retaliation capabilities includes enough nuclear warheads to wipe out 400 million people in the Soviet Union and China within 30 minutes' time.[4]

Today the United States, Great Britain, France, Russia, China, and India already have atomic weapons. Israel, South

Africa, and Germany likely have the atomic bombs as well. And it probably won't be long before almost any well-funded dictator in the oil-rich Middle East will have nuclear warheads at his disposal. As the clock ticks onward, it is only a matter of time until the inevitable disaster strikes.

The Final Blast

The Bible predicts the final devastation of the earth in "one hour" (Revelation 18:10). That's what is said about the destruction of the prophetic "Babylon," the symbolic name for the kingdom of the Antichrist. The Bible says, "All your riches and splendor have vanished, never to be recovered" (Revelation 18:14). Even the merchants and sailors will not come near this land, but will "stand far off, terrified at her torment," and cry out, "In one hour such great wealth has been brought to ruin!"(Revelation 18:15,17).

The apostle Peter provides an even more vivid description of the final blast that will devastate this planet when he warns, "But the day of the Lord will come like a thief. The heavens will disappear with a roar; the elements will be destroyed by fire, and the earth and everything in it will be laid bare" (2 Peter 3:10).

Bible teacher John Phillips notes that Peter's prophecy of a great end-times conflagration of the earth and its atmosphere uses precise terminology that accurately describe a nuclear explosion. Phillips observes that the "elements" (Greek, *stoicheia*) are defined by Liddell and Scott's *Lexicon* as "the components into which matter is divided" (or atoms) and the term "dissolved" (Greek, *luo*) comes from the basic Greek word meaning "to loose" that which is bound (as in nuclear fission). The term "great noise" (Greek, *rhoizedon*) is found nowhere else in the New Testament and signifies "a rushing sound as of roaring flames." The term "fervent heat" is derived from the Greek medical term *kausoo,* denoting a fever. But Peter's use of it in application to inanimate objects is the only such known usage anywhere in Greek literature. Thus, Phillips concludes, "Peter described in accurate terms the untying of the atom and the resulting rushing, fiery destruction which follows it."[5] "That day will bring about the destruction of the heavens by fire, and the elements will melt in the heat" (2 Peter 3:12).

ECOLOGICAL DISASTERS

Destroying the Earth

During the Persian Gulf War, vast amounts of oil were spilled into the Persian Gulf. That was one more in a series of ecological disasters in humanity's war against the earth, which *Time* magazine called "eco-war."[6] The environmental carnage in the Gulf War resulted in burning oil refineries, bombed-out chemical plants, and the largest crude oil petroleum dump in the history of the world. As Iraqi troops set Kuwait's oil refineries ablaze, they also apparently dumped millions of gallons of crude oil into the shallow waters of the Persian Gulf at Kuwait's supertanker loading pier, the Sea Island Terminal.

Ecological experts have called it the worst environmental damage ever done to the earth. Because of the enclosed geographical features of the Persian Gulf, whose only outlet to the sea is the 35-mile-wide Strait of Hormuz, the gulf is especially vulnerable to ecological warfare. Hussein's cruel attack on the environment turned the "mother of all battles" against the earth in a perverse act of environmental terrorism.

But the deterioration of the earth's resources goes far beyond a giant oil spill. Air pollution is so bad in many of the earth's industrial cities that it is becoming a major problem for future survival. The gradual evaporation of the ozone layer higher up in the earth's atmosphere could result in more severe forms of skin cancer than have ever been known before. Radiation leaks, like the one at Chernobyl in the former Soviet Union, could spell major disaster for the inhabitants of earth.

Interestingly, the Bible prophesies that God's judgment will include "destroying those who destroy the earth" (Revelation 11:18). Prophecy expert Dave Hunt observes, "A number of

God's judgments are ecological in nature, devastating the grass and trees and polluting oceans and rivers."[7] The Bible predicts terrible ecological disasters in the last days of the Great Tribulation before Christ returns to spare the world from total destruction.

Problems in the Environment

The oil war in the Middle East reminded us all of the continuing problems related to our mismanagement of the earth's natural resources. Lack of strategic oil reserves and the continued gluttonous consumption of oil by the industrial giants will eventually deplete our supply.

Then there is the destruction of the Amazon rain forests, which has been called "one of the great tragedies of history."[8] What is at stake in the Amazon is the greatest supply of oxygen in the whole world. Now years of assault by builders, developers, and settlers have endangered the supply. Philip Fearnside of Brazil's National Institute for Research in the Amazon says, "Unless things change, the forest *will* disappear."

While Third-World countries need to use their resources for their own economic growth and development, they must do so with measured caution. When the efforts for advancement turn into environmental rape, everyone loses. We need only to consider countries like Haiti, where greedy men have stripped away the natural resources and left an environmental catastrophe in their selfish path.

Bible prophecy points to the end of the world as a day when the natural environment of the earth is devastated. The seas and rivers of earth are described as blood and we are told that every living creature in the sea will die (Revelation 16:3). The air will become so thick that no one can see the sun, and yet people are "seared by the intense heat" (Revelation 16:9). While we can only *assume* what this means, it certainly sounds like the aftermath of a disastrous nuclear war.

A Global Economic Network

In recent months it has become abundantly clear that the global economy is fast replacing individual national economies. What happens on the stock market in Tokyo early in the day has a domino effect on the trading floors of London and New York later in the same day. With the instantaneous communication systems available to us via telephones, fax machines, computers, and even satellite telecasts, the world is now at our doorstep. Economic isolation is a thing of the past.

Economic cooperation is becoming the name of the game in Europe. In 1992 the continent-wide deregulatory movement kicked into high gear, forming the New Europe. The twelve members of the European Economic Community (EEC) removed most of the trade barriers and internal regulations that have separated their countries for centuries. The end result will be a European passport and driver's license valid in all EEC nations. This will spur international travel on the continent where an invigorated European market with the free flow of money, goods, services, and workers has the potential to become the world's economic giant. The EEC headquarters in Brussels, Belgium is the central nervous system of the New Europe, whose motto is: "Many Tongues, One Voice."

The EEC had its beginnings in the democratic alliance of Belgium, the Netherlands, Luxembourg, Italy, France, and West Germany. By 1973 it also included Denmark, Ireland, and Great Britain. Greece joined in 1981, and Spain and Portugal brought the membership total to 12 in 1986. The recent reunification of East and West Germany made Germany the dominant player in the EEC. And the democratization of the formerly communist nations of Eastern Europe opens vast potential for the growth of the European giant. Jean Monnet, the original architect of the EEC, said that the economic community itself was "only a stage on the way to the organized world of tomorrow."[9] Europe, then, stands ready to unite again for the first time since the sixteenth century and the Holy Roman Empire of Charles V.

Interestingly, *Europe* magazine reported that the basic silver coins of the European currency will have twelve stars and a bust of Charles V imprinted on them.[10]

A unified political federation in Europe seemed like an impossible dream in 1957, but now it appears to be a future reality. Even powerful Margaret Thatcher was swept out of office for resisting the tide of popular support for the EEC. We can only *speculate* whether the EEC has anything to do with the prophecies of a global economy in the last days. Revelation 13:17 tells us that no one will be able to "buy or sell unless he had the mark, which is the name of the Beast or the number of his name." Whatever the mark of the Beast is, this passage implies that no financial transactions can occur without it.

A CASHLESS SOCIETY

We can only speculate about how we will become a cashless society. Years ago, prophecy authors envisioned people with numbers branded on their heads or hands. Today's writers believe that these may be "invisible" computer codes indelibly "tattooed" on the body for computer identification. There is nothing wrong with such speculation if it is healthy, creative, and helpful—and if we don't preach it as *fact*. The Bible does not mention computers, but it now seems plausible that they may have a role in the cashless transactions mentioned in Revelation 13:17. However, it's possible that 20 years from now something else will come along; technology races ahead faster than we realize.

For instance, several years ago I picked up Delta Airlines' *Sky* magazine and read a fascinating article entitled, "Electronic Money Will Change Your Life."[11] In the article, the author explained that one day every bank in America would be linked up to the same central computer and that "electronic funds transfer systems" would eventually lead to a "cashless society" dependent on "paperless transactions." He talked about credit and debit charges for the purchase of merchandise at point-of-sale terminals and the automatic deduction of monthly payments from a person's bank account.

Those concepts seemed rather farfetched at the time. Even the author admitted it would take the general public time to get used to these ideas. He suggested that "1995 is a fair guess." My, how time flies!

In the emerging global economy, the ideas that are connected to national economies, interests, and corporations are taking a back seat. Robert Reich, Clinton cabinet member and former Harvard professor, has observed that "the very idea of an American economy is becoming meaningless, as are the notions of an American corporation, American capital, American products, and American technology. A similar transformation is affecting every other nation, some faster and more profoundly than others."[12]

In light of the expanding world economy, conventional discussions of gross national product and national economic growth are no longer viewed as crucial to our national health. Yet, Reich observes that it was the prosperity of the American economy that shut down communism and contained the Soviet menace. "America led the way toward a global capitalism modeled on American capitalism," he notes in his most recent book.[13]

Certainly, the success of the American free enterprise system and our multinational corporations have set a standard for economic success around the world. Yet it may be this very success that has propelled Europe to create its own economic system rather than being annexed to ours. In the gradual shift from high-volume production to high-tech and high-value goods, the global web was set to catch us all. Thus, Reich concludes, " 'American' corporations and 'American' industries are ceasing to exist in any form that can meaningfully be distinguished from the rest of the global economy."[14]

AMERICA IN TROUBLE

Pat Robertson has warned that "the economies of Europe

and Japan may equal or exceed the economy of the United States during this decade."[15] We certainly seem headed in that direction. Only a renewed commitment to the values of hard work can reverse the trend that now seems so inevitable. Chuck Colson and Jack Eckerd have raised this same issue in their powerful book, *Why America Doesn't Work.*[16] They raise the questions:

> Why doesn't America work? Because for too long too many of us have waited for someone else to do something. . . . Can we make America work— restore our productiveness and competitive place in the world, raise responsible young people, and clean up the mess in our inner cities and prisons?

Their answer is an emphatic *yes.* But they warn:

> Make no mistake: The key is to restore a high and morally rooted view of work that once again inculcates in the American character those historic values of the work ethic—industry, thrift, respect for property, pride in craft, and concern for community.[17]

Christianity has always been a working man's religion. From the carpenter shop in Nazareth to the fishing boats of Galilee, Jesus and His disciples were working-class men who knew what a hard day's work was all about. The early Christians displayed such a commitment to work that the apostle Paul said, "If a man will not work, he shall not eat" (2 Thessalonians 3:10). But such values have all too often been lost in our welfare-dependent society.

Congressman Jack Kemp is correct when he says, "America doesn't have just one economy—we have in reality two economies, separate and unequal. Our second economy—the welfare economy—is more akin to the Third World Socialist economy than to the capitalist West."[18] He is absolutely right!

The welfare system has taken away the people's incentive to work, while increasing federal spending at almost every level.

Belief in individual responsibility has shifted to a belief in social responsibility, which in turn has overburdened the tax system, encumbered governmental agencies, and slowed our economic growth. We have already produced second- and third-generation welfare families. Our whole welfare system is founded on the faulty premise that the working population must support what is becoming an increasingly larger non-working segment of our society. During the past 20 years, the number of citizens living on welfare has increased 500 percent. Unless this trend is reversed and the dignity and decency of work is restored, we will have little hope of competing in the world market.

WHOSE WORLD ORDER?

The idea of a New World Order really isn't all that new. The Roman poet Virgil penned it in Latin centuries ago: *Novus Ordo Seculorum,* meaning a "new order of the ages" or a "new world order." Charles Thompson, designer of the Great Seal of the United States, placed it under the pyramid with the eyeball that appears on the back of a one dollar bill. Thompson, a member of the Masonic order, served as secretary to the Continental Congress that adopted the seal in 1782.[19]

Over the years various leaders from Woodrow Wilson to Nelson Rockefeller to Jimmy Carter have talked about a new world order of global peace and politics. *The Humanist Manifesto II* (1973) called for the limiting of national sovereignty and the building of a "new world order." In recent years the concept of a New World Order has become a prominent theme in the New Age movement.

Elliot Miller, a former New Ager, describes the New Age movement as a metanetwork of loosely knit organizations bound together by a common vision of a coming new age of peace and global enlightenment.[20] This network includes 1) the consciousness movement (mind expansion), 2) the holistic health movement, 3) the human potential movement, 4) and occult mysticism. In addition, various environmentalists and peace organizations are also a part of the New Age movement.

All New Agers believe in *monism,* the philosophy that "all is one." This is the basis for their belief that man is divine. The religious authority within the movement is based upon mystical experiences like reincarnation, channeling, and altered consciousness. Ultimately, New Agers believe personal transformation will lead to planetary transformation. Miller notes that "while retaining strong elements of humanism, naturalism and existentialism, New Agers have simply gone on to spiritualize the universe by making consciousness its essence, rather than matter."[21]

New Age fads include crystals, pyramids, psychic fairs, "channeling" the voices of departed spirit-guides, and "cosmic convergences." For the most part, New Agers are anti-nuclear activists, ecology-oriented planetarians ("save the planet"), and political utopians. Leading proponents have included futurist Alvin Toffler, biologist Jonas Salk, physicist Fritjof Capra, psychologist Elizabeth Kubler-Ross, actress Shirley MacLaine, and Mark Satin, author of *New Age Politics.*

It is in the area of its political vision that New Agers talk of a New World Order. New Age activism has given rise to the so-called "green movement" worldwide. In general, New Age politics vigorously promote the idea of a united global community that stands against materialism and industrialization. They also promote abortion on demand, children's rights to leave home at any age without parental approval, the right to die, and a host of left-wing political ideas all in the name of human freedom.

Most New Agers reject biblical Christianity and the idea of a sinful human nature as cultural "myths." Thus salvation, as Christians understand it, is unnecessary. Miller warns that New Age politics could easily lead to a "politics of repression" resulting from a naive utopianism and an overly optimistic view of human nature.[22] To the New Agers' humanitarian views, nationalism appears to be division of the world family. While we who are Christians also have high regard for human life and are concerned about global peace and interaction, we do not hold physical survival as the dominant spiritual value.

The degree to which the New Age movement can shape the vision of a New World Order remains to be seen. But one thing is certain—New Agers are getting their message across loud and clear. We need only to visit the bookstores in the local mall to see how many New Age titles are selling like hotcakes.

A NEW AGE CONSPIRACY?

Ever since Constance Cumbey wrote *The Hidden Dangers of the Rainbow* in 1983, many Christians have viewed the New Age movement as a secret conspiracy attempting to overthrow evangelical Christianity.[23] Cumbey argued that the "Aquarian Conspiracy" was destined to enthrone the New Age Christ (Maitreya, actually the Antichrist).

Cumbey predicted the elimination of orthodox religions; forced redistribution of the world's wealth; mass planetary initiations; disarmament campaigns; and the increased display of New Age symbols such as the rainbow, Pegasus, the unicorn, the all-seeing eye of Freemasonry, and triple sixes.

Cumbey proposes a conspiracy theory linking New Agers, the Illuminati, humanists, the Trilateral Commission, the Council on Foreign Relations, secret societies, and the occult. She also implicates everyone from the late Nelson Rockefeller to Henry Kissinger, Jimmy Carter, and George Bush as dupes of the conspiracy.

I certainly agree that various groups, such as the eighteenth-century Illuminati, had designs on a new world order, but such designs have yet to materialize in any significant manner. I have been a Christian for over 40 years now and have been told that the Illuminati was about to take over the world at any moment throughout those 40 years. But it has never happened!

Many Christians are somewhat naive in their understanding

of international politics and thus are easily susceptible to believing conspiracy theories that have little basis in fact. It is as though these same Christians want to believe theirs is the terminal generation and the Antichrist and the False Prophet are already meeting in some secret chamber plotting the overthrow of the world at any moment. I certainly believe that time is running out and Christ could come to rapture His church at any moment. But I also believe we have a responsibility to show caution in the area of prophetic speculation.

I am convinced Satan is too clever to expose his own grand design as easily as might be expected. Rather, he influences the "spirit of the age"—those inexorable forces that seem to be moving in a particular direction. These forces color how we view the issues of our time and even our moment in history.

For example, the popular mindset prior to World War I was one of confrontational *nationalism* that led to The Great War. Prior to World War II, it was *expansionism* that plunged Germany and Japan into devastation. Today it is *globalism*. While many people, groups, movements, or ideologies may contribute to such trends, it is more likely that Satan himself is the "master of the game." Rather than look for a definable human conspiracy behind it all, we should probably take a behind-the-scenes look at the great spiritual conflict of our time.

SPIRITUAL WARFARE

Despite the hopes and dreams of a New World Order of peace and prosperity, we must not forget the reality of spiritual conflict behind the scenes of human events. The Bible reminds us that when people cry, "Peace, peace," there often is no peace. In commenting on the ultimate spiritual struggle between God and Satan, John MacArthur writes, "The very fact that tragedies exist is not contradicting proof that a good and loving God is responsible for them, but rather evidence that some other personal being is actively engaged in trying to stifle the plan of God."[24]

The Old Testament describes Satan as the deceiver of the nations (Isaiah 14:12-16). In the New Testament, Satan is pictured as one who perverts God's Word (Luke 4:9-12), hinders God's servants (1 Thessalonians 2:18), and accuses the brethren (Revelation 12:10).

Throughout the New Testament, Jesus confronted the power of Satan and his demons. Spiritual warfare is a constant topic of the New Testament Gospels and epistles. New Testament scholar Ralph P. Martin writes, "The spiritual hierarchy of evil is depicted . . . in terms of principalities and powers."[25] But Jesus Christ is depicted as superior to all principality and power (Colossians 2:10). He is seen as triumphing over all principalities and powers and overcoming the power of Satan (Ephesians 1:21).

The apostle Paul refers to the heavenly conflict with "spiritual forces of evil in the heavenly realms" (Ephesians 6:12). I believe such spiritual conflict is a reality. We cannot explain hideous atrocities, such as the Nazi Holocaust, apart from demonic influence. While we must be careful not to overestimate Satan's power, neither should we underestimate it. I cannot believe the prince of darkness is going to lie down and let the world go merrily on its way to peace and prosperity.

The world has obviously come to a great crossroads today. On the one hand, everyone is talking democracy, capitalism, peace, and prosperity. But on the other hand, old hatreds, fears, and jealousies continue to divide the world into a patchwork quilt of ethnic rivals and bitter enemies. The decisions made today will determine the course of world events in the years ahead. But democratization alone, without a spiritual awakening, will only result in empty materialism. And no matter how hard the nations try, they cannot build a new world order without God. Therefore, the struggle for world dominion will remain a constant reality.

Chapter 7

❦

THE STRUGGLE FOR WORLD DOMINION

We have now moved to the final round in the struggle for world dominion. The collapse of communism has removed one of the significant players in what one writer has called the "Great Millennial Endgame."[1] But the end of the Cold War is by no means the end of the struggle for world supremacy. As we approach the third millennium of church history, we may well be running out of options—and time!

Everyone realizes that we are standing on the edge of a new day in world politics. The dramatic changes we have witnessed in Europe, the Middle East, and the former Soviet Union tell us that the world is undergoing a massive transformation. The aftermath of World War II finally has been shaken from us like an old rag. Eastern Europe is awakening to a new day of hope and freedom.

At the same time, there is great concern about where all these changes are taking us. Charles Colson recently said, "We sense that things are winding down, that somehow freedom, justice, and order are slipping away. Our great civilization may not yet lie in smoldering ruins, but the enemy is within the gates. The times seem to smell of sunset."[2] He goes on to suggest that Western civilization is facing the greatest crisis encountered since the barbarians invaded Rome.

Robert Hughes, in a recent essay on "The Fraying of America," observes that we are a society "obsessed with therapies and filled with distrust . . . skeptical of authority and prey to superstition."[3] He reminds us it was just over 50 years ago that W.H. Auden foresaw our day through the eyes of Herod in *For the Time Being.* In this fascinating portrayal, Herod muses over the unpleasant task of slaughtering the innocent children at Bethlehem in order to eliminate Christ. Herod rationalized that if he allowed the Christ child to escape, "reason will be replaced by revelation. Objective rational law will be replaced by subjective visions . . . of a New Age."[4]

REASON ABOVE REVELATION

Ironically, that is exactly where life in the 1990s has gone. Our neglect of God's revelation has pushed us to the limits of our own rationalization. We have abandoned rationality for irrationality in the attempt to hold onto belief in something—anything—beyond ourselves.

All through the twentieth century, we have allowed godless secularism to replace the Judeo-Christian values of our society. God has been deliberately and systematically removed from prominence in our culture and in our intellectual lives. We have made Him irrelevant to our culture. Tragically, we have also made our culture irrelevant to God. In so doing, we have abandoned our spiritual heritage. The Christian consensus that once dominated Western culture is now shattered. The world is already mired in the quicksand of secularism, relativism, and mysticism. It is a wonder we have survived as long as we have.

We should not be surprised, therefore, that spiritual confusion is rampant. Almost daily someone launches a new religion, predicts the end of the world, or announces himself to be the Messiah. Is it any wonder that a nonbelieving world shakes its head and walks away?

In the place of biblical Christianity, people are now calling for a New World Order that consists of the very elements Scripture warns will signify the empire of the Antichrist:

1. *World Government*

    Globalists are now insisting that national governments should surrender their sovereignty to a one-world government. Such a government would operate through a world headquarters, a world court, and even a world military.

2. *World Economy*

    This aspect of globalism is already upon us. No developed nation of any kind can survive today without networking with the global economy. There is almost no such thing as an "American" product that is not dependent on parts, trade, or investments from foreign countries.

3. *World Religion*

    This will be the final phase of the New World Order. The idea of a new world religion of peace and cooperation is already being proposed. Religious unity has been endorsed by Pope John Paul II, the Dali Lama, and leaders of the World Council of Churches.

What we are witnessing today may well be the fulfillment of the biblical prophecies of the end times. Peter Lalonde sees a parallel between the predictions in Revelation 13 and the current move toward a New World Order.[5] These Scripture passages predict the rise of a powerful world ruler who is able to control the world politically and economically. This ruler will have at his side a false prophet who promotes a one-world religion.

Lalonde writes, "It is breathtaking to realize that what we are witnessing today in the emergence of the 'New World Order' may well be a fulfillment of Revelation 13! In the world's rejection of the true Prince of Peace and in their rush to build their own earthly kingdom, the Antichrist's government is being fabricated for him!"[6]

A New World Order

Former President Bush observed, "A new partnership of nations has begun, and we stand today at a unique and extra-ordinary moment . . . out of these troubled times . . . a New World Order can emerge."[7] When George Bush met with former Soviet leader Mikhail Gorbachev on Malta in 1989, *Time* magazine flashed the startling headline: "Building a New World Order."[8] In his historic meeting with Pope John II, Gorbachev admitted, to "having embarked upon the road of radical reform . . . [and] crossing the line beyond which there is no return to the past."[9]

Former Jesuit scholar Malachi Martin has suggested that the struggle for the New World Order will come down to three major powers: Western capitalists, Eastern socialists, or the Catholic Church. Martin observes, "There is one great similarity shared by all three of these geopolitical competitors. Each one has in mind a particular grand design for one-world governance."[10] Martin theorizes that just as the Soviet Union lost its hegemony in Eastern Europe, so also will the United States lose its hegemony in world politics. Then and only then, Martin suggests, will the Pope make his move toward world dominion.

The Fall of Communism

Undoubtedly, the most dramatic event of our lifetime has been the sudden and apparent collapse of the Soviet Union. Mikhail Gorbachev's policy of *glasnost* ("openness") toward democracy brought down the Berlin Wall and the Iron Curtain all in one fell swoop. The former Soviet leader's willingness to release the East European satellites did not protect a reformed communism within the Soviet Union; rather, it opened the floodgates for cries of freedom within the Soviet Union as well.

By Christmas Day of 1989, communism lay dead in the streets of Eastern Europe. Germany was talking reunification; East and West Berliners were dancing in the streets; Poland was getting ready to elect Lech Walesa as president; and Romania's Nicolae Ceausescu, the last of the communist dictators, was executed in Bucharest. In a startling moment, the flash of history streaked by and Eastern Europe was free at last!

This was Gorbachev's great gamble in the "millennial endgame." By letting the satellites go, he hoped to communicate that he was concentrating on improving the Soviet economy at home, but alas, the strategy failed. The smell of freedom was being blown by the winds of change all the way to Moscow.

The Soviet citizens wanted more—much more! They, too, wanted to be rid of the dreaded system that had enslaved them for nearly 75 years. Public demonstrations began to mount against the government. Soon, upstart Boris Yeltsin was elected president of Russia and Gorbachev was forced to share the political spotlight with him. Then came the foiled coup attempt in August, 1991. The Communist party hard-liners made one last desperate attempt to hold onto their power by kidnapping the Soviet leader. But millions of people jammed Red Square and shouted allegiance to Yeltsin.

The military backed down. The coup failed because of a lack of popular support from the people. Ironically, the very movement that began as a people's revolution ended the same way. The people themselves stood up and demanded democracy and freedom, and to the surprise of the whole world, the people won! The "Evil Empire," with all its KGB agents, sinister intentions, nuclear weapons, and military might fell in one week to the people themselves.

Communism had impoverished every facet of individual life—spiritual values, human rights, social programs, and the economy. People had simply had enough and said so! Their spontaneous grass-roots revolt was like a gale-force wind hurtling across Eastern Europe, knocking down every obstacle to democracy.

The New Europe

Today there is a new wave of optimism sweeping across Europe. By the end of 1992, the economic unification of the

European Community became complete. "We are past the point of no return," announced Jacques Delors, the father of European unification.[11] The Europe of the future may well become a political union, the United States of Europe. If this happens, Europe, not America, will be the strongest and most powerful "nation" on earth—economically, politically, and even militarily. And if the current European Community were to continue to expand into the former Soviet satellites of Eastern Europe and even into Russia itself, Europe would stretch from the Atlantic Ocean to the Pacific Ocean for the first time in history!

The key players in the New Europe will be England, Germany, and Russia. The unification or cooperation of these three superstates could well determine the issue of who controls the world of the future. Already Chancellor Helmut Kohl of the reunified Germany is calling for Germany to "take a bigger role . . . in the community of nations."[12]

As Germany struggles to reassert her leadership on the Continent, at least one writer has observed, "With the collapse of the Soviet Union and its empire, the logic behind Germany's subordinate role . . . has also collapsed, and the postwar balance of power on the European continent has been upset."[13] What role Germany will play in the future remains to be seen. Some see her taking a passive role in international politics. Others fear the rise of the "Fourth Reich."

The new Soviet Union, the Commonwealth of Independent States, could also emerge as a major player in European politics. It is still too early to tell how the new order of this part of the world will shape up or if Yeltsin's government will even survive. While the label "Soviet Union" may be gone, the reality still remains. The vast land of 250 million people with hundreds of thousands of nuclear weapons still exists.

Many Christians believe that the resurgence of the New Europe fulfills the biblical prophecies of a revived Roman Empire in the last days. Like the architects of the Tower of Babel, advocates of the New World Order believe that "coming together" will consolidate what were formerly volatile or weak economies and foster global peace and cooperation. Helmut Kohl has said, "The United States of Europe will form the core of a peaceful order . . . the age prophesied of old, when all shall dwell secure and none shall make them afraid."[14]

The real tragedy in all this talk of global unity is the absence of any emphasis on the spiritual roots of democracy and freedom. The gospel has been blunted in Western Europe for so long that there is little God-conscientiousness left in the European people. Without Christ, the Prince of Peace, there can be no hope for manmade orders of peace and prosperity. There will be no Millennium without the Messiah!

In the present configuration of nations, the Islamic world seems out of step with all the talk of a New World Order. They seem to have only one agenda: an Islamic World Order. There is little or no room in Islam for pluralism on religious or political issues. Muslims believe they are right and all others, including Christians and Jews, are infidels.

WHERE ARE WE NOW?

What is now more clear than ever is that we have taken a quantum leap toward the fulfillment of the biblical prophecies of the last days. The stage is now being set for the final climatic act in the long history of the human drama. Things could not have been arranged more perfectly to set the stage for the fulfillment of the prophecies of the end times:

1. The fall of communism has paved the way for a *world economy* and a *world government*. The global web is tightening around us every day.
2. Secularism is giving way to *New Age mysticism* as the do-it-yourself religion of our times. The end result will be the watering down of religious beliefs so that they are more palatable to the general public.
3. Global economic interdependence will eventually lead

to a *global political system* that dominates national sovereignty.

4. *Materialism* and *selfism* will replace spiritual values. Mankind will be left in the mindless pursuit of material prosperity as the basis for meaning and value in life.

5. The *spiritual vacuum* that results will leave the world ready for the ultimate deception: The Great Lie of the Antichrist that will deceive the whole world.

6. A *world leader* will quickly arise on the international scene promising to bring peace and economic stability. He will receive the support of the European community and eventually control the whole world.

7. A *crisis in the Middle East* will trigger this world leader's intervention militarily and politically. He will eventually sign a peace treaty with Israel, only to break it later.

8. A *False Prophet* of international fame will suddenly emerge to gain control of the world religious system and use it to reinforce the worship of Antichrist.

9. All resistance to the world system will be crushed by a massive *worldwide persecution*. Men, women, and children will be slaughtered in the name of the World State.

10. *Israel* will become the central figure in the conflict with the World State. The Antichrist will eventually break his covenant with Israel and invade her land, setting the stage for the Battle of Armageddon.

How Close Are We to the End?

There is no doubt in my mind that we are fast approaching the final chapter of human history. The hoofbeats of the four horsemen of the Apocalypse can now be heard in the distance. The stage is set for the final act of the human drama. The clock is ticking away the last seconds of any hope for a reprieve. We are being swept down the corridor of time to an inevitable date with destiny.

How much time is left? Only God knows! I believe we must use every means at our disposal to preach the gospel of God's saving grace everywhere we can while there is still time. This is not the time to rest on our laurels. Rather, we have a window of opportunity, by the grace of God, and we need to take advantage of it right now! It is time for us Western Christians to take seriously our responsibility to evangelize the world in our lifetime.

We have prayed for a spiritual breakthrough in the Iron Curtain for the past 75 years. Now that it has come, we must respond by mobilizing workers, financial resources, printed materials, and broadcasting equipment to get the gospel into what is still the greatest bastion of atheism on our planet.

If we do not meet this challenge and fulfill our obligation, every kind of false religious cult, every kind of secular materialism, and every kind of moral perversion will rush to fill that vacuum. We alone have the truth that can set men and women free from the chains of spiritual oppression. We must be willing to do all we can to fill that void—now!

Jesus Christ said what we all must realize at this crucial hour: "As long as it is day, we must do the work of him who sent me. Night is coming, when no one can work" (John 9:4). To the ancient church at Philadelphia, our Lord said, "I have placed before you an open door that no one can shut" (Revelation 3:8). God has also given today's church an open door to preach the gospel where it has not been heard for a long time. May we rise to the occasion, recognizing that the ultimate struggle for world dominion is between the forces of Christ and the forces of Satan.

Chapter 8

⟨∿⟩

CAN THERE BE PEACE
IN THE MIDDLE EAST?

It was the handshake seen round the world: The Israeli Prime Minister and the Chairman of the Palestine Liberation Organization shaking hands on the White House lawn. And all the world was watching by television wondering if this new treaty will really work. The handshake was the symbolic culmination of several months of secret negotiations between the Israelis and the Palestinian Arabs.

Two simple letters signed by the late Israeli Prime Minister Yitzhak Rabin and PLO Chairman Yasser Arafat marked the beginning of a new hope for peace in the Middle East in September 1993.[1] Both agreed to recognize the other's right to exist in peace and security. And before it was all over, they were celebrating in an elaborate ceremony on the outskirts of ancient Jericho.

"Enough of blood and tears," Rabin announced. "Today we are giving peace a chance."

Within a few months, King Hussein of Jordan joined the peace process. But still there were detractors. Hard-liners in

Gaza protested with strikes and street riots. Iran denounced the peace effort as "a treacherous step." Syria remained cautious, still insisting on its rights to the Golan Heights. Other Arab nations took a wait-and-see position.

The rest of the world was amazed. Lifelong enemies making peace? Could it be for real? Will it last? Henry Kissinger called it a "fairy tale" come true. "It was one of those rare occasions on which hope suspends all doubts," he wrote. "Neither I nor anyone else present will ever forget the anguish and hope in the nearly biblical remarks of Prime Minister Rabin. Nor could one fail to be affected by the culmination of Arafat's torturous journey."[2]

As noble an effort as the Rabin-Arafat "peace" may have been, it has been extremely difficult to maintain. Rabin himself was later assassinated by an Israeli extremist opposed to the peace process. Israel's present prime minister, Benjamin Netan Yahu, is opposed to "land for peace" negotiations. Tensions remain high on the West Bank and in the Gaza Strip. Constant protests by Palestinians and Israelis alike make the political future doubtful.

Many people believe the only permanent solution to the ongoing conflict will be a peace treaty backed up and enforced by a powerful military leader who will bring the world back from the brink of disaster.[3] A Middle East peace settlement is clearly predicted in Daniel 9:25-27, and other prophecies from this passage have already been fulfilled. Daniel predicted the rebuilding of Jerusalem "in times of trouble" (verse 25), which was done in the days of Nehemiah. He then looked down the corridor of time and saw the Anointed One (Messiah) "cut off" (verse 26). Looking even farther, beyond the death of Christ, Daniel predicted, "War will continue until the end" (verse 26). And so it has!

THE PROSPECT OF PEACE

The intensity of the Arab-Israeli conflict goes deeper than just the Palestinian question over the issue of control of Israel's occupied territories. Certainly this is an important issue in the current debate, but the wanton attack on Israel by Iraq during the Persian Gulf War shows a deeply embedded hatred that will not easily be resolved. This points to the need for a peaceful settlement of gigantic proportions.

The prophet Daniel predicted the rise of a future world leader who will sign a peace treaty ("covenant," Daniel 9:27) with Israel, presumably for seven years. But he will break that agreement at the halfway mark and attack Israel. While Bible scholars have debated the interpretation and application of this passage for centuries, it seems to speak of an era not unlike our own. Daniel tells us of a future age when knowledge and travel will increase (Daniel 12:4); he seems to have a global picture in mind.

Daniel also predicted an alliance of ten nations growing out of the old Roman Empire (Daniel 7:7-14), symbolized by the ten horns of the creature that represents the last world system. Walvoord suggests, "The final confederacy of ten nations will constitute the revived Roman Empire, which will have the economic and political power necessary to control the Mediterranean."[4]

The unification of the European Economic Community (or Common Market) in 1992 signaled a serious step in the direction of a global economy. This EEC dream, which called for the eventual economic and political union of the United States and Europe,[5] has been a long time coming since it was first proposed after World War II and formalized by the Rome Treaty in 1957. Since Bible prophecy points to a final economic, military, and political giant that sits on seven hills (i.e., Rome), we have to wonder if we are not now witnessing the coming together of the final alignment of the nations at the end of the age.

IRRECONCILABLE DIFFERENCES

The great tragedy of the ongoing crisis in the Middle East is that without Christ, there is no hope of lasting peace. Men may talk of peace, plan for peace, and work for peace, but there will be no peace. The irreconcilable differences between the Arabs and the Jews go back 4,000 years. These old hatreds and prejudices will not go away as a result of mere human efforts. No amount of education, psychology, social welfare, or government planning can eradicate that unresolvable hatred. It can be corrected only by the love of Christ.

During the church age, all people, including Jews and Arabs, are called to faith in Jesus Christ, the Prince of Peace. Only in Him can there be lasting peace between mortal enemies. In Christ, all men are equal brothers. There is neither Jew nor Arab nor Gentile. We are one in Christ.

This great truth bonds the hearts of all Christians, no matter what their national or ethnic origin. In Christ, no one group is better than another. No one person takes precedence over another. All are equal in Christ. It was this truth—that a slave and a master were equal brothers in Christ—that broke the bond of slavery in the Roman world. When we kneel before Christ and submit to His lordship, we find that the ground is level at the cross.

This leaves the Christian in a precarious position, however. On the one hand, he is to preach the gospel to all people, including Arabs and Jews. He is to love them both with the love of Christ. On the other hand, most Christians believe that God is not finished with His people Israel. He still has a plan for their future after the times of the Gentiles have been fulfilled. Therefore, these Christians sympathize with Israel's right to exist as a people and a nation.

This tension calls us as servants of Christ to love two peoples who do not love each other. We must demonstrate the power of the gospel to both groups. It is not easy to affirm Israel's right to her land without offending Arabs. And it is not easy to express concern for the Palestinians without offending the Israelis. But we must—for Christ's sake and the gospel.

Christians must also guard against the temptation to hate Arabs, or any Muslims, because of the war in the Middle East.

It is possible to rightly affirm the just cause of war as a response to injustice without hating our enemies. This is not easy to do, especially when we have lost loved ones to that enemy. Despite the Persian Gulf War and the problems that stemmed from it, we must pray that God will give us grace not to hate the Iraqis but to demonstrate the love of Christ to them.

AN INEVITABLE DESTINY?

One of the tragedies of the Persian Gulf War is the widening division between some of the Arabs and some people in the West. Though we have demonstrated that cooperation is possible and Western and Saudi flags have flown side by side, there is still a deep resentment toward the United States within the hearts of many Arab peoples.

Some people have speculated that the current crisis has set the prophetic stage for the future.[6] The Western world is calling for a peaceful resolution of the conflict. This will require greater cooperation between Arabs and the West. Yet the old hatreds remain deeper than ever. The barbaric cries of, "Death!" to all who oppose the Arabs do not give much hope to a lasting, peaceful solution.

This is the great dilemma that has confronted the Jewish people for centuries. They have often tried to live at peace with their Muslim neighbors.[7] History attests to the fact that Jewish communities often flourished among the Arabs—in Egypt, Syria, Iraq, and Iran. But sooner or later, the Jews came under persecution and often forced to flee for their lives.

Thus future Arab-Israeli relations are very much in doubt. The Jews were without a national home for nearly 2,000 years after the Romans destroyed Jerusalem in A.D. 70. For centuries they were forced to live among Christians and Arabs alike as they wandered the earth in search of a home. Finally, in 1897, an Austrian Jew named Theodore Hertzl cried out to the leaders of Europe. "There is a land without a people," he said, "and there is a people without a land. Give the land without a people to the people without a land."[8] Hertzl wrote the book *Judenstat,* which called for the rebirth of the State of Israel. At the same time, he convened the World Zionist Congress in Switzerland to discuss his hopes and plans for the future.

Later on, British General Allenby took Jerusalem from the Turks without firing a shot on December 9, 1917. The Turks had allied with the Germans during World War I and their losses included Palestine. The British passed the Balfour Declaration, which called for the establishment of an independent Jewish state in Palestine. On May 24, 1920, the League of Nations ratified Britain's mandate over Palestine and opened the door for Jews to return to their ancient homeland.

A SIGNIFICANT PROPHECY FULFILLED

Many Christians believe that the Jewish people's return to Palestine is the most significant evidence of fulfilled prophecy in our time. John Phillips says, "It is one of the greatest signs of the end times."[9] He points to Isaiah 60:9-10 as dramatic testimony to this prophetic fulfillment: "Surely the isles shall wait for me, and the ships of Tarshish [Europe] first, to bring thy sons from far. . . . And the sons of strangers shall build up thy walls, and their kings shall minister unto thee" (KJV).

When the United Nations met to vote on the partitioning of Palestine on November 27, 1947, there was little hope of Israel getting the necessary two-thirds vote. At the last minute, the Soviet Union surprised everyone and voted *for* the establishment of the State of Israel and the vote passed! On May 14, 1948, the British High Commissioner for Palestine stepped down and the Zionist Council in Tel Aviv proclaimed the State of Israel established with David Ben Gurion as prime minister and Chaim Weizmann as president.

Several Arab states, including Egypt, Jordan, and Iraq, immediately proclaimed a holy war against the newly reborn Israel and attacked on all sides. But to the world's great surprise, Israel not only defended itself but also forced the Arabs to accept a truce. In 1956 Nasser of Egypt tried to attack Israel and was decisively turned back. In 1967, Nasser provoked the Israelis into the Six-Day War. By the time it was over, Israel had conquered the Sinai, the old city of Jerusalem, the West Bank, and the Golan Heights. Israel's military superiority shocked the secular world. But Bible scholars recalled the prophet's predictions that the Jews would "never again . . . be uprooted from the land I have given them" (Amos 9:15).

By 1973 Anwar Sadat was in power as Egypt's president. His independence became clear when he threw a group of Russian military advisers out of the country. But increased tension over the oil embargo lingered. Sadat caught the world by surprise when he attacked the Sinai peninsula while Syria attacked the Golan Heights on October 6, 1973—Yom Kippur, the Jewish Day of Atonement. Again the Israelis won a decisive victory, but this time with heavy losses.

In the years that followed, Sadat made an incredible statesmanlike move and traveled to Israel to meet with Prime Minister Menachem Begin and to address the Knesset, the Israeli congress at Jerusalem. Later, Begin and Sadat met with American President Jimmy Carter in 1978 at Camp David, Maryland to discuss the Camp David Peace Accords. Their goal was to establish a lasting peace in the Middle East. In March of 1979 Israel and Egypt signed a formal peace treaty in Washington, D.C. A leading Arab nation had committed itself to peace with Israel!

THE ESCALATING DRAMA

In the meantime, major changes were under way throughout the Middle East. Muammar Qaddafi took over Libya, nationalized its oil industry, and began threatening to carry out acts of international terrorism. The United States responded with brief but effective military action. In 1979 an Islamic revolution in Iran overthrew the Shah and brought the Ayatollah Khomeini to power in a newly established Islamic republic.

Over in Iraq, Saddam Hussein came to power and launched a territorial disputes war with Iran from 1980 to 1988. A cease-fire came in August of 1988. Then two years later, in August of 1990, Hussein invaded Kuwait and brought the wrath of the United Nations down on Iraq. Later, in 1992, Yasser Arafat began talking seriously about a peace treaty between Israel and the PLO.

In many ways, Israel's survival in the midst of a sea of Arabs is indeed miraculous! While we could speculate that Israel's presence in the Holy Land may be only temporary, that seems unlikely. The Jewish people seem to be there to stay. Many, including prophecy expert and author Dr. John Walvoord, chancellor of Dallas Theological Seminary, believe "the times of the Gentiles" (Luke 21:24) may be coming to a close and the great end-times drama is about to unfold.[10]

God promised Abraham that He would bless them that blessed him and curse those who cursed him (Genesis 12:3). Many Christians view this promise as binding on nations and how they treat Israel. The prophet Jeremiah put it even more strikingly when he said, "All who devour you [Israel] will be devoured; all your enemies will go into exile. Those who plunder you will be plundered; all who make spoil of you I will despoil" (Jeremiah 30:16).

Whatever a person's view of eschatology, he must admit that Israel has suffered unjustly at the hands of her neighbors. To be sure, the Arabs have genuine concerns for which we can sympathize. But unreasonable acts such as Iraq's unprovoked missile attacks against Israel certainly do not make sympathizers out of most Americans or Europeans. Nor do such acts of terrorism commend the Islamic faith to the rest of the watching world.

CRIES FOR PEACE

There is something shocking and horrifying about war that makes us all shudder. The highway to death, its ultimate finality, makes it terrifying. So much so that in the midst of every war, the cries for peace begin to surface. We would think that modern, educated people would avoid the destructiveness of war at all costs. But there is something basically destructive in the psyche of human depravity that makes war an inevitable reality.

All over the world, efforts are constantly being made to stop conflicts and propose settlements for opposing parties. This has been an especially difficult prospect in the Middle East, where underlying tensions go back for centuries and where religious issues provoke bitterness, hatred, and even war. That is why a proposed peace settlement in the Middle East raises such high hopes. It promises an end to hostilities and the beginning of a new order for the future.

The immediate solution would seem to be a peace treaty "that settles disputes, disarms antagonists, and provides absolute guarantees," writes Walvoord.[11] Such a treaty would probably be backed up by military force, but whatever settlement is reached will only be temporary in nature. Conflicts are bound to resurge again and again.

THREATS OF WAR

The Bible promises both peace and war in Israel's future. The Old Testament Scriptures indicate that a great world leader will come onto the scene promising lasting peace in the Middle East. He will sign a peace treaty with Israel. Most Christians believe this leader will arise from the European Economic Community, though some think he may be from the Middle East itself.

We can only *speculate* at this point as to how that peace settlement may come about in the near future. The continued threat of war, an economic crisis, or an oil shortage could all be factors in triggering further conflict in the Middle East. Whatever the cause, the call for peace will outcry the call for war. The Bible predicts a treaty (covenant) between Israel and a powerful world leader that will result in peace and prosperity for the nation and people of Israel (Daniel 9:27).

But this peace will be short-lived—only three and one-half years. For in the middle of Daniel's prophetic seventieth week, the world leader will break his covenant with Israel. Many Christians believe this will happen at the midpoint of the seven-year tribulation period. Once the world leader has deceived Israel, he will turn against the people in a violent persecution for another three and one-half years. Jesus called this time the "great tribulation" (Matthew 24:21 KJV). Jeremiah called it "the time of trouble for Jacob" (Jeremiah 30:7). The Scriptures indicate that God will use the Great Tribulation to awaken Israel to the truth about their Messiah.

In Israel's most desperate hour, the Lord Jesus, the Prince of Peace, will return to spare Israel and bring His resurrected bride, the church, back with Him to rule in His millennial kingdom on earth. Jesus Himself warned, "If those days had not been cut short, no one would survive" (Matthew 24:22). But God, in His great wisdom and mercy, has promised to spare the world for a better future when there will be peace for 1,000 years while our Lord reigns in Jerusalem upon the throne of David.

SETTING THE STAGE FOR THE END

The Old Testament prophets predicted that the Jews would eventually return to the Promised Land and that Israel would be reestablished as a nation before the end of the times of the Gentiles. Jesus predicted, "Jerusalem will be trampled on by the Gentiles until the times of the Gentiles are fulfilled" (Luke 21:24). It would seem that time is running out for the Gentiles and that the stage is now set for the end times.

It is always possible that the end is hundreds of years into the future, but it is not very probable. The precarious nature of international events and the ever-present threat of nuclear war remind all of us how near the end could actually be.

It is also possible that Israel's present return to the Holy Land will end in failure and that the Jewish people will be expelled only to return again later in fulfillment of prophecy. But with circumstances being what they are, that is not very probable. It seems unlikely that He would not choose to use the present-day setting to bring about the end that Jesus and the prophets predicted.

The exact timing of last-day events may be indefinite, but several prophetic elements are now in place:

- Israel is back in the Promised Land for the first time in nearly 2,000 years.
- The Arab nations seem bent on driving Israel into the Mediterranean Sea.
- The intervention of the major Western powers in the Middle East indicates the times of the Gentiles are still operable.
- Attempted peace settlements, though desirable, seem destined to failure in resolving the Arab-Israeli conflict.
- Popular resentment against Israel among the Arab peoples is deeper than ever since the Persian Gulf War.
- Iraq's attempt to rally the Arabs into a *jihad* ("holy war") against Israel shows how quickly an Arab coalition could form and invade Israel in the end times.
- The political unification of Europe seems more likely than at any other time in recent history. This may fulfill Daniel's prophecies of a great end-times revived Roman Empire.
- The stage is now set for a prominent world leader to arise from the West and promise peace for the entire world.
- A global economy is now upon us. It is only a matter of time until the whole world is one economic unit waiting to be taken over by a sinister power.
- The potential of nuclear war remains an ever-present reality in the world's march to Armageddon.

While we must be careful not to set dates or to speculate

irresponsibly, we certainly can discern that time is running out for our world. Man's clever ingenuity has bailed him out of disaster on numerous occasions during the Cold War years of the late twentieth century. But humankind may be running out of options. It may all be over sooner than we think!

Chapter 9

⚬⚬⚬

RIPS IN THE ISLAMIC CURTAIN

The beliefs and prejudices of Islam are deeply entrenched. It is often pictured as a religion of fanatics, terrorists, and warmongers. While this is not a fair picture of Islam on the whole, it is true of a radical element within the Muslim faith. This radical element causes most Westerners to be repulsed by Islamic concepts of justice, revenge, and so-called "holy wars."

The "Islamic Curtain" cuts off the Arab world from outside influences. "Behind that wall of prejudice," Dave Hunt observes, "any religion except Islam is forbidden."[1] Political leaders see themselves as protectors of Islam. Converts to Christianity are often persecuted, imprisoned, and even executed. In many Islamic countries, Christians have been put to death by their own families! Gospel preaching is outlawed and gospel literature is banned from public distribution. Freedom of the press, of speech, and of public assembly is forbidden.

The Koran, the sacred book of Islam, advocates the killing of apostates and unbelievers. Muhammad himself led several battles in which many people were killed. He claimed that God had called him to spread Islam with the point of the sword. History tells us that Muhammad's followers swept across the Middle East and North Africa, conquering everyone in their path. They crossed into Europe and took Spain, but they were finally turned back by Charles Martel in the Battle of Tours in France in A.D. 732. Even today it is considered an honorable duty for Muslims to kill Christians and Jews.

Hunt is correct when he writes, "It is impossible to understand the current situation in the Middle East, much less anticipate probable future developments there, except in the context of the religion that grips and motivates the Arab world."[2] This is a world of diverse peoples held together by the bond of a common religion, Islam, and a common language, Arabic. Together, these elements have a viselike grip on the Muslim world.

This is not to say that the Arab people have not made significant contributions to the world in art, literature, architecture, mathematics, and science. The intricate geometric designs of Islamic art are among the most beautiful in the world. The Arab people themselves can be kind, loving, and hospitable. We must be careful not to close the door of the gospel to them by failing to love them for the sake of Christ. But when it comes to religion, there is something demonic about their hatred of Jews and Christians.

We must remember that it is the Arabs who have insisted on destroying Israel at all costs. Israel has never declared such intentions against her Arab neighbors. If there is going to be real and lasting peace in the Middle East, the Arabs must change their stated policy and be willing to coexist with Israel.

A NEW ERA OF WARFARE

As the bombs began bursting over Baghdad at 12:50 A.M. Iraqi time on January 17, 1991, President George Bush summoned Marlin Fitzwater, his press secretary, to the White House. Fitzwater read the president's official statement to the assembled press at 7:06 P.M., on January 16 in Washington, D.C. He announced, "The liberation of Kuwait has begun."

The era of modern televised warfare had also begun. For the next several days, Americans and much of the rest of the world sat transfixed by live telecasts that were instantly relayed by satellite from such distant places as Baghdad, Iraq; Riyadh, Saudi Arabia; Amman, Jordan; and Tel Aviv and Jerusalem, Israel. The era of global communications had been with us for some time, but suddenly we were experiencing it firsthand. For the first time in history, we could watch people use live television as a two-way communications system. Instead of a day-old videotape carried by jet from Vietnam, we were watching Tom Brokaw, Dan Rather, and Peter Jennings talking live with correspondents all over the world.

The instantaneous nature of mass communication brought the distant conflict right into our living rooms. The public seemed captivated, however, not only by the war itself, but by the ominous prospect which it seemed to foreshadow—the possibility of a nuclear holocaust in the Middle East. Indeed, it seemed to many people that Armageddon was on our doorstep.

When Saddam Hussein ordered the invasion of Kuwait on August 2, 1990, he unleashed the guns of August that would result in the bombs of winter beginning in January 1991. At a time when the world wanted to congratulate itself for ending the Cold War and ushering in a new order of peace and prosperity, Hussein upset the global balance of power.

After the Persian Gulf War erupted, a friend told me, "It all sounds like the replay of some ancient biblical drama." Then, reflecting for a moment, he wondered if the war might not have prophetic significance. "Isn't Iraq ancient Babylon?" Tom asked. "Do you suppose this could lead to something like Armageddon?"

Questions like these began to grip the hearts of believers and nonbelievers alike. "Iraqiphobia" spread like a plague. Fears of poison gas attacks, chemical and biological warfare, and even nuclear destruction reminded the world that its frail attempts at a lasting peace are limited by human depravity—greed and the lust for power.

The vulnerability of our own lives is always challenged in a time of war. We are forced to look more deeply at the basic issues and ultimate realities of life. Despite the beauty of this earth and the affluent quality of our lives, war shockingly reminds us that this life is still a "vale of tears." Our real destiny is in the dust. And somehow the world sensed that quickly as news about war engulfed the media.

Soon the world's newspapers began screaming their headlines: "Geneva Peace Talks Fail" (January 10); "War in the Middle East" (January 16); "U.S. Bombs Baghdad" (January 17); "Israel Hit by Missiles" (January 18). Satellite-relayed telecasts gave us front-row seats for the greatest television drama ever—a live war in the Middle East.

War in the Middle East! Israel under attack! It sounded all too familiar to those of us raised on Bible prophecy. "Could this really be Armageddon?"some wondered.

"I can't believe this is actually happening right before my eyes!" a friend exclaimed.

"Things are happening so fast that I bet even Hal Lindsey[3] is confused!" a pastor told me with a gleam in his eye.

Other people wondered what all the talk about a New World Order meant. "It sounds to me like we've come down to the end and it's about all over," a Sunday-school teacher suggested to me. "The Antichrist is almost certainly alive—biding his time, awaiting his cue," one well-known Bible teacher exclaimed.[4]

A Line in the Sand

The blitz of Kuwait on August 2, 1990, by Iraq's combat-hardened troops and tank convoys overthrew the tiny nation and sent its royal family scurrying into exile. Saddam Hussein had taken the biggest gamble of his military career and refused to withdraw. Intelligence reports convinced President George

Bush that Hussein fully intended to bring Saudi Arabia under his control as well, leaving himself as the oil kingpin over 62 percent of the world's oil reserves. Such a position would have enabled Hussein to tip the world's balance of power in whatever direction he wanted.

World reaction to Hussein's virtual rape of Kuwait came quickly and decisively. At Saudi Arabia's request, the United States immediately sent thousands of troops to secure the Saudi-Kuwait border and halt any further aggression by Iraq. The Security Council of the United Nations passed 12 resolutions against Iraq and demanded immediate withdrawal and the restoration of Kuwait's legitimate government. Bush met Soviet President Mikhail Gorbachev at Helsinki, Finland, in September 1990, and they issued a joint statement calling on Iraq to withdraw unconditionally from Kuwait. Bush then began building a 28-nation multinational coalition against Iraq in what would become the most massive military buildup since the Vietnam War.

By late November 1990, the United Nations Security Council voted 12-2, with China abstaining, to authorize force to liberate Kuwait and set January 15, 1991, as the date by which Iraq must withdraw or face punitive action. For the first time since the Korean War, 45 years earlier, the United Nations had authorized military action against an aggressor nation.

In reaction to the United Nations' sanctions and demands, Saddam Hussein refused to negotiate or withdraw and called for an Arab holy war (*jihad*) against the demons from the West. George Bush had drawn a "line in the sand" at the Saudi border and warned Iraq that its aggression would not be rewarded. When last-minute efforts for a resolution were rebuffed by Iraqi Foreign Minister Tariq Aziz at Geneva, Switzerland on January 9, 1991, the stage was set for war in the Middle East.

"THE MOTHER OF ALL BATTLES"

Saddam Hussein, the father of all rhetoric, warned the Western powers that the "Mother of All Battles" was about to begin. Like many Muslim leaders, he began to salt his political speeches with religious terms while appealing to three major Arab themes: poverty, piety, and the Palestinians. He denounced the Kuwaitis for their wanton wealth, proclaimed George Bush the Great Satan, demanded the reinstatement of the Palestinian state, and called for a holy war against the United Nations coalition that was demanding his withdrawal from occupied Kuwait. In a final gesture of twisted piety, Saddam ordained that *Allahu Akbar* (God is Great) be sewed onto the Iraqi flag.

In the strange metaphysics of war, Hussein became a master of disguises, erupting forth in a dozen moral charades. Always attempting to use the media to his advantage, he often miscalculated public response. The raids on Israel provoked international outrage, as did his parade of battered American POWs and the ecological disaster caused by the great oil spill in the Persian Gulf. Finally, in the face of certain defeat he said, "If this is martyrdom, let it come . . . the alternative is humiliation!"

On January 16, 1991, George Bush faced America in the most-watched event in television history and announced, "Tonight the battle has been joined . . . and we will win!" In that address he also added, "We have before us the opportunity to forge for ourselves and for future generations a New World Order, where the rule of law, not the law of the jungle, governs the conduct of nations."

LIVE FROM THE MIDDLE EAST

The eyes of the world were riveted on the first war in the age of global information. It all began right in the middle of the television networks' evening newscasts and held the world spellbound over the next several days. Various American reporters provided an unprecedented live account of the war from inside the enemy capital. As the bombs burst overhead, ABC correspondent Gary Shepard in Baghdad announced, "An attack is under way." So was the greatest television drama of all time.

Three CNN reporters on the ninth floor of the Al Rashid Hotel—Bernard Shaw, Peter Arnett, and John Holliman—provided a live report of the start of the war. This reminded older generations of Edward R. Murrow's live radio broadcasts from London during the Nazi blitz. "Something is happening outside . . . we're getting star bursts in the black sky," Shaw reported.

"They're coming over our hotel. You can hear the bombs now," Arnett announced to the stunned world.

"This feels like the center of hell," Shaw added.

Meanwhile, the television networks canceled all regular programming and provided continuous coverage for the next 42 hours. President Bush's speech on Wednesday night, January 16, drew the biggest audience in television history—61 million households. Then the bombardment of information began. The public was deluged with facts about the war. In the next several hours, we learned about Scud missiles, Tomahawks, Patriots, mobile-launchers, cruise missiles, surgical bombing, carpet bombing, F-15s, M1s, cluster bombs, laser-range finders, smart bombs, and even the TOW 2 (Tube-launched Optically traced Wire-guided) antitank missile. We were given live reports by military experts, retired generals, political analysts, Middle East experts, world leaders, local politicians, and eyewitnesses.

Then, in what *Time* magazine called "another quirk of timing oddly fitted for the TV age, the drama often heated up just as the prime-time hours approached."[5] On Thursday night viewers watched with nervous apprehension as correspondents in Jerusalem and Tel Aviv relayed reports of Iraqi missiles hitting Israel. NBC's Martin Fletcher in Tel Aviv conducted his live report while wearing a gas mask that served as a precaution against a possible chemical attack.

These images will long remain in our minds. Like the John F. Kennedy assassination or the space shuttle explosion, their impact transcended every other thing happening in our lives at that moment. Most of us will never forget where we were or what we were doing when it all began. I had just finished a four-night Bible study series at a church in St. Louis, Missouri. We cut short the last night so we could all gather around a television set in a parlor to watch the president's speech. It was an incredible moment as the seriousness of the specter that lay ahead gripped us all.

AN EYE ON PROPHECY

The unprovoked Iraqi attack on Israel angered the civilized world. Emotional support for the Jewish nation rose immediately and dramatically. Iraq's indiscriminately launched "to whom it may concern" Scud missiles blasted Tel Aviv's civilian neighborhoods, bringing havoc and destruction. People who were familiar with biblical prophecy had even greater images flashing through their minds. "Could this be the Battle of Gog and Magog or even Armageddon?"one stunned housewife asked as we stared ominously at the television report.

Certainly, war in the Middle East ought to get our attention. For anyone who takes the Bible seriously, there can be little doubt that the Gulf War brought us another step closer to the return of Christ. "If God wanted to set the stage for the end, He couldn't have done it any better," one prophecy scholar told me recently.

John Walvoord, former president of Dallas Theological Seminary, notes: "The rapidly increasing tempo of change in modern life has given the entire world a sense of impending crisis."[6] He too raises the difficult questions about how long the world can survive until a madman has nuclear bombs or how long the world economic struggle can be held in check before it ends in a bloodbath.

During the Gulf War, the world was sitting on the edge of its seat. The entire global community was transfixed. They were ready for any possibility—chemical or nuclear warfare. Then the war ended as quickly as it had begun.

After 40 days of Allied bombing from the air in over 100,000 sorties, the ground war finally started. To the world's surprise, it was all over in 100 hours! The greatest tank war since World War II left 90 percent of Iraq's tanks captured or destroyed. Nearly 100,000 Iraqi soldiers surrendered to the Allies; many of them were starving or destitute. Rather than the final battle that many people thought it might be, Operation Desert Storm was only a microcosm of Armageddon yet to come.

The greatest lesson students of prophecy can learn from the Gulf War is that we dare not assume more than the Bible actually predicts. The *facts* of prophecy are clear, but the *assumptions* we draw from those facts and the *speculations* we make off those assumptions are another matter. Just because the end is *near* doesn't necessarily mean the end is *here*.

WAR AGAINST THE WORLD

A recent magazine article by Benjamin Barber in *The Atlantic* pointed out that the attitude of *jihad* is one of "retribalization," which pits one culture against another and one people against another.[7] Barber calls this "retribalization of large swaths of humankind by war and bloodshed—a threatened Lebanonization of national states . . . a Jihad in the name of narrowly conceived faiths against every kind of interdependence . . . social cooperation and civic mutuality."

Interestingly, Barber draws a parallel between the opposite, but equally dangerous, tendencies of globalism ("McWorld") and tribalism ("Jihad"). He writes:

> The tendencies of what I am here calling the forces of Jihad and the forces of McWorld operate with equal strength in opposite directions, the one driven by parochial hatreds, the other by universalizing markets, the one re-creating ancient subnational and ethnic borders from within, the other making

national borders porous from without. They have one thing in common: neither offers much hope to citizens looking for practical ways to govern themselves democratically.[8]

In the modern world, the great problem for the Muslim mind is pluralism. It is a struggle for Christians as well. Both Christians and Muslims struggle with the relationship of their faith to a nonbelieving world. We who are Christians believe we must live the lifestyle of Christian discipleship before the unbelieving world as a testimony of God's grace in our lives. We do not believe in forcing others to accept our faith.

Islam, as I understand it, is quite different. The attitude of many Muslims is to spread their faith by the sword or kill the infidels who reject it. Tragically, this often leads to a breakdown of civility that results in international "gang war."

Ironically, *jihad* is a word that generically means "struggle," referring to the struggle of the soul against evil. In this regard it is a legitimate concept that Christians, Jews, and Muslims share. But when it is applied to religious war in the name of God, *jihad* becomes an ugly and frightening concept that seems to condone terrorism and mass murder in the name of religion. Here Christians and Jews part company with Muslims. We do not believe in forcing other people to accept our faith, neither at swordpoint nor gunpoint.

THE LAST *JIHAD*

Tragically, the prophet Ezekiel predicts an invasion of Israel in the last days by a host of Arab nations (Ezekiel 38-39). This prophecy was given centuries before the rise of Islam, yet it names Persia (Iran), Cush (Sudan/Ethiopia), and Put (Libya) as part of the invading force along with Gomer (Cimmerians from the Russian steppes) and Beth Togarmah "from the far north" (Turkey).[9]

This alliance is headed by Gog, the "chief prince" of Magog.

Much has been said about the identification of Magog. The ancient Jewish historian Josephus (*Antiquities* 1.123) identified this by the Greek term "Scythians" (barbarians from the northern frontiers). Alfonso III of Spain (A.D. 866-910) interpreted Ezekiel's prophecy as depicting the defeat of the Moors (Muslims) in Spain. Other people have seen Magog as the Huns, Mongols, Magyars, Turks, or Russians.

The *Scofield Reference Bible* (1909) stated that Magog was Russia, and the communist revolution of 1917 helped that identification to remain popular in evangelical Christian circles. It must be carefully admitted, however, that Scofield's identifications were based on limited records available to nineteenth-century scholars like Keil and Delizsch. While the older records are similar to more recently discovered records, they are not identical. Magog may well designate the barbaric hordes from Southern Russia, but this is an *assumption* based on *limited facts*. Other identifications in Ezekiel's prophecy, such as "chief prince" (Hebrew, *rosh*) being the root word for Russia, "Meschech" being Moscow, "Tubal" being Tobolsk, and "Gomer" being Germany, are almost totally rejected by modern scholars and linguists.

Here is a case in point for distinguishing the *facts* of prophecy from the *assumptions* and *speculations* drawn from them:

Fact. Magog, Persia, Cush, Put, Gomer, and Togarmah will invade Israel in the last days and be destroyed (Ezekiel 38-39).

Assumption. We can identify these ancient peoples as modern-day Russia, Iran, Sudan/Ethiopia, Libya, and Turkey.

Speculation. Russia and her Arab allies will invade Israel during the tribulation period and be destroyed. Even as careful a scholar as Walvoord states this as though it were fact.[10]

Yet there is nothing in Ezekiel 38-39 about the tribulation period. This is generally *assumed* because the invasion described by Ezekiel follows the predicted regathering of Israel in Ezekiel 37.

Meschech (*Muski*) and Tubal *(Tabal)* are also mentioned in Ezekiel 32:26 in reference to an alliance with the hordes of Egypt, Assyria, and Elam, but most prophecy commentators do not believe this passage has any future significance.

The prophet Jeremiah predicts an invasion of Babylon by "Ararat, Minni and Ashkenaz" (Jeremiah 51:27). The name "Ararat" refers to the mountain where Noah's ark rested after the Flood and appears in Isaiah 37:38 and 2 Kings 19:37 as "Armenia" in the KJV, following the Septuagint. Yamauchi notes that the biblical name "Ararat" is cognate with Urartu, the mountainous region north of Assyria which was home to the people who proved to be a formidable rival to the Assyrians in the eighth century B.C.[11] These people settled the region later known as Soviet Armenia. "Ashkenaz" is the Hebrew equivalent of the Akkadian name for the Scythians, *Ishkuza*. The general term "Scythian" designates the nomadic tribes from the Russian steppes.

If Ezekiel's prophecy does not square with any *known* biblical or historical invasion, then we can *assume* it has not yet taken place. That being the case, twentieth-century evangelical Christians have often assumed that the Bible is predicting a Russian-Arab alliance against Israel in the last days. This may well occur, but it is only an assumption at best.

Let me digress for a moment and do some *speculating* of my own. Let's assume Ezekiel is predicting an event that is still in the future—an event in which certain nations will form an alliance against Israel. Since we know that Iran, Libya, Turkey, Sudan, and Ethiopia are all Muslim (or Muslim influenced), could it not be possible that the Muslim republics of the southern part of the former Soviet Union are in view in this prophecy and not necessarily Russia itself?

Many people do not realize that the former Soviet Union

was made up of 15 different republics, of which Russia was only one. Also, most Americans are unaware that one citizen in five in the former Soviet Union is Muslim. These Muslims live in the republics of Kazakhstan, Uzbekistan, Turkmenistan, Tadzhikistan, Kirgizia, and Azerbaijan. If the current movement toward independence were to continue, these Muslim republics could eventually break away from Moscow altogether. Several Muslim political parties have been formed with this agenda. These Soviet Muslims could join a last great *jihad* ("holy war") against Israel in an alliance with other Muslim states. This could fulfill Ezekiel's prophecy and not even involve Russia itself.

I make this suggestion based on pure *speculation*. I have never seen this idea put forth in print by prophecy prognosticators. During the anticommunist era, it was more exciting for people to assume the Bible predicted the destruction of Russia. It's possible, however, that Scripture is predicting the destruction of a last Muslim *jihad* against Israel. Imagine the reaction throughout the Muslim world if Israel were to attempt to rebuild the temple in Jerusalem. If that were to happen, you can be sure the Muslim world would vigorously oppose the Israeli efforts.

IRAQ'S ROLE IN THE FUTURE

It's interesting to note that in Ezekiel's prophecy, Iraq (Babylon) is not listed among the nations invading Israel. Could this mean that Iraq will be destroyed or taken over by another nation such as Iran? Any answer to this question is pure *speculation*. Prior to the British conquest of the Turks during World War I, Iraq's territory was part of Turkey's Ottoman Empire. In reality, if Iraq could claim it owned Kuwait, Turkey could claim it owns Iraq.

Mesopotamia (Iraq) was conquered by Muslim Arabs in the seventh century A.D. Then under the Abbasid caliphate, Baghdad was made the imperial capital in about A.D. 750. Later,

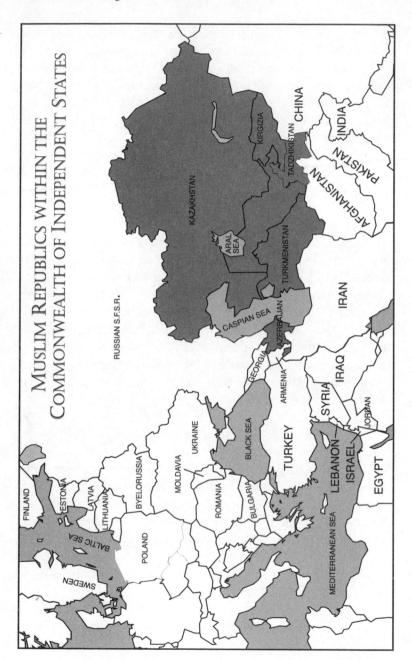

MUSLIM REPUBLICS WITHIN THE COMMONWEALTH OF INDEPENDENT STATES

the Seljuk Turks established rule over Iraq in A.D. 1055 and continued to have a dominant influence in the following centuries despite brief interludes of Mongol and Persian control.

From the conquest of Suleiman the Magnificent in 1534 until World War I, the Turks had virtual control of the Middle East. In 1914, the British landed at Basra (Iraq), but were unsuccessful in conquering the Truks until the archaeologist-adventurer T.E. Lawrence ("Lawrence of Arabia") persuaded Sharif Hussein of Mecca to revolt against the Turks. Baghdad fell to the British and Saudi forces in 1917. Sharif Hussein later became the king of Saudi Arabia and his son Faisal became king of Iraq in 1921. In 1958, Iraq federated with Jordan, which was ruled by another descendant of Sharif Hussein. But a succession of military revolts led to a series of revolutionary governments that finally resulted in the Arab Socialist Renaissance (Ba'ath) Party coming to power in 1968.

Throughout the Ba'ath control of Iraq there has been a great deal of interest in emphasizing the ancient history of Babylon. Frequent attempts have been made to identify Iraqi sovereignty with the past greatness of ancient Babylon. But it was Saddam Hussein who determined to use this interest to build a monument to himself.

WILL BABYLON BE REBUILT?

Charles Dyer, author of *The Rise of Babylon*, argues that Iraq will rebuild the ancient city of Babylon and even includes pictures in his book that show the limited reconstruction that has been done at the site of the ancient ruins under Saddam Hussein's authority.[12] Dyer then *speculates* that Babylon will be rebuilt, become the dominant city in the Middle East, and finally be totally destroyed in fulfillment of the prophecies of Isaiah 13:1-22 and Jeremiah 50:1-42.

While this is certainly possible, it is also highly improbable. Bible scholars have been almost unanimous in their belief that the prophecies of Babylon's fall were fulfilled in ancient times and serve to foreshadow the fall of the symbolic "Babylon" of the future (Revelation 14–18). Gleason Archer writes, "This fall of Babylon is prophetically typical of the overthrow of latter-day Babylon."[13]

Dyer argues that the prophecies about Babylon's fall refer to a violent and total overthrow. "Babylon . . . will be overthrown by God like Sodom and Gomorrah. She will never be inhabited or lived in through all generations" (Isaiah 13:19-20). When Babylon fell to the Medes and Persians in 539 B.C. under Cyrus the Great, it did fall in one night, but Dyer says it was not a violent destruction. The prophet Daniel was in Babylon at the time and predicted its overthrow to King Belshazzer (Daniel 5), and saw it happen that very night.

The Fall of Babylon

There is more to the fall of Babylon than some people realize. It should be noted that Cyrus of Persia had crossed the Tigris River as early as 547 B.C. and conquered the kingdom of Lydia, whose capital was Sardis (the same Sardis that appears in Revelation 3:1) and whose king was the wealthy Croesus (known to the Greeks as Midas). In the meantime, Cyrus turned south and began sacking the cities of Babylonia until eventually Babylon itself was cut off and besieged. Nabonidus the ruler of Babylon fled, leaving Belshazzar, the co-regent, in charge. That explains why Belshazzar offered to make Daniel the "third highest ruler" in the kingdom when Daniel had interpreted the mysterious handwriting on the wall of the royal palace (Daniel 5:29). Belshazzar himself was only second in command.

Babylon fell the same night that the writing on the wall appeared during Belshazzar's wild drinking festival; this festival is also mentioned in the works of the ancient historians Herodotus and Xenophon. Herodotus also attributed the fall of Babylon to the Persians' clever idea of diverting of the Euphrates River, which protected the city. This permitted the Persian and Median troops to enter the city along what was now a dry riverbed.[14] Isaiah's reference to the Medes (Isaiah

13:17) and his later prediction about the rise of Cyrus (Isaiah 44-45) have led most evangelical Christian commentators to assume the prophecy of Babylon's fall was fulfilled initially in the one-night capture of the city by the Medes and Persians.

Cyrus then appointed a governor, Darius the Mede (Daniel 5:30), over the city of Babylon. Cyrus himself was killed in battle in 530 B.C. and buried in a tomb that still stands at Pasargadae, the ancient Persian capital. He was succeeded in turn by Cambyses II (ruled 592-522 B.C.) and Darius the Great (ruled 521-486 B.C.), who extended the borders of the Persian Empire. Darius spent his winters at Babylon and appointed his son Xerxes (the Ahasuerus who married Esther [see Esther 1:1]) as his personal representative in the ancient city. Xerxes later ruled from 485 to 465 B.C. and conducted several expeditions against the Greeks.

It was under Xerxes that Babylon revolted against its Persian overlords. Xerxes responded harshly in 482 B.C. and attacked the city, demolishing its fortifications and burning the temple of Marduk (chief god of Babylon) to the ground. Thus, the biblical prophecy of Babylon's demise was further fulfilled. Babylon still existed, but it was a shell of what it had once been. Any influence that Esther, a descendant of Jewish captives, may have had on her husband's decision to attack Babylon is pure speculation.

The Attempts to Rebuild Babylon

When the Persian Empire finally fell to Alexander the Great of Macedonia in 331 B.C., Alexander resolved to make Babylon his eastern capital. He put 10,000 soldiers to work clearing the debris left by Xerxes and rebuilding some of the structures that had been destroyed. But his disastrous campaigns to Bactria (Afghanistan) and India left him exhausted, and he died in Babylon on his return trip to home on June 13, 323 B.C. After that Babylon's fate was left to Alexander's generals, the *Diadochi* (successors). With Alexander's death, the plans for rebuilding Babylon died as well. God protected His prophecy from being contradicted.

In 312 B.C. Seleucus, one of Alexander's generals, captured the remains of Babylon, which had been virtually destroyed by ensuing struggles for its control. Unwilling to rebuild the devastated city, Seleucus founded a new city in 305 B.C., named for himself, Seleucia-on-the-Tigris, about 90 kilometers north of Babylon. Eventually the remaining civilian population of Babylon was forced to move there by Seleucus and his successor, Antiochus I (ruled 281-261 B.C.).[15]

During the Hellenistic period, Babylon was reduced to a village, with nearby Esagila maintained as a religious site. One last attempt to rebuild Babylon to its former glory was made by the infamous Antiochus IV Epiphanes, who founded a Greek colony there in 173 B.C., complete with a theater and gymnasium. Ancient cuneiform texts hail Antiochus as "Founder of the City" and the "Savior of Asia." He was the same ruler who conquered Jerusalem and desecrated the temple during the intertestamental period. He appears in Bible prophecy as a type of the Antichrist (Daniel 11:36-45).

In time, the Seleucid kings lost control of Babylon to the Parthians. One of the Parthian rulers, Mithradates I, conquered Babylon in 141 B.C. Another, Himerus, destroyed the city and its temples in 123 B.C. The Parthians moved their capital to the city of Ctesiphon, across the Tigris River from Seleucia, leaving Babylon in ruins. By 24 B.C. the Greek geographer Strabo described Babylon as empty and desolate. Though a small Jewish community existed there during Roman times, it was later totally abandoned. When the Roman Emperor Trajan stopped there in A.D. 116, he found nothing but ruins.[16] Left behind was the largest mound of ruins in ancient Mesopotamia (modern Iraq), covering 340 acres. Thus the name Babylon, once associated with greatness and splendor, came to refer to great ruins. The city that fell in one night eventually decayed into the sands of time. The Hebrew prophets were right and their predictions were fulfilled.

Some Key Facts about Babylon

Those who have predicted the rise of Babylon during the

end times point out that the prophets predicted Babylon's walls and towers would be torn down (Jeremiah 50:15; 51:30), that Babylon "will never be inhabited" (Isaiah 13:20), and even her stones will be left untouched (Jeremiah 51:26). Dyer argues that those prophecies have not been fulfilled because small populations have been found near Babylon at various times since the Middle Ages. He also notes that German archaeologist Robert Koldewey found people quarrying the city's ancient bricks when he arrived in 1902 to excavate the mound.

The interpretation of Bible prophecies about Babylon has been discussed at great length by theologians of all types. Dyer argues that a literal fulfillment of the prophecies of Babylon's fall has not occurred; therefore, he *assumes* Babylon will play a significant role in end-time events along with a revived Roman Empire. He therefore views the "Babylon" of Revelation 17 as the "literal rebuilt city of Babylon."[17] From this assumption, Dyer *speculates* that the rise of Saddam Hussein in Iraq and his attempt to rebuild Babylon has prophetic significance.

This "Two Babylons" theory is not new. It has been proposed before, but has not been taken very seriously. Dyer is to be commended for arguing his case carefully and thoroughly, but there are several problems with it. The most important is the failure to view the Babylon of Revelation through first-century A.D. eyes. To first-century people, Babylon was no longer an active or significant city. It had already fallen!

1. *Ancient Babylon has already been destroyed*

Archaeological and historical records clearly attest to both the conquest and destruction of ancient Babylon, leaving it in total ruins. General statements, like every stone being discarded, cannot be pressed to literal extremes. Besides, bricks made of clay are not stones. In addition, Jesus Himself said of the Temple Mount at Jerusalem that "not one stone here will be left on another; every one will be thrown down" (Matthew 24:2). Yet the Wailing Wall, comprised of the foundation stones of Herod's Temple Mount, is still standing today.

Jesus' prophecy was fulfilled when the Romans destroyed Jerusalem in A.D. 70 and tore down the temple. That a few stones remained standing does not cancel the fulfillment of the prophecy. The structure of the temple came down just as Jesus said it would. To over-literalize prophecy is to miss the intent of the prophecy.

2. *Babylon has never returned to her former glory*

Babylon's ruins are ample testimony to the fulfillment of the prophecies against it. It has been uninhabited for nearly 2,000 years. A few squatters on its fringes do not negate the fact that the greatest city of the ancient world was in fact destroyed as the Hebrew prophets predicted. Saddam Hussein's attempts to refurbish the ancient mound are nothing more than a tourist trap and monument to his own exaggerated opinion of himself. While he may view himself as the modern successor to Hammurabi and Nebuchadnezzar, the rest of the world sees him quite differently.

It is highly unlikely that Saddam Hussein or anyone else will rebuild ancient Babylon into a major end-time evil empire only to have it permanently destroyed again.[18] In fact, God may have used the Gulf War to keep Hussein from rebuilding Babylon and protect the prophecy so that Babylon will not be rebuilt. Saddam, like Alexander the Great and Antiochus Epiphanes before him, has seen his hopes shattered.

3. *Isaiah and Jeremiah prophesied against ancient Babylon*

Those who believe Iraq will rise to greatness, rebuild Babylon, and finally be destroyed tend to view Isaiah 13 as a future event when people "come from faraway lands" (Isaiah 13:5), namely, the United States, to destroy Iraq. A person could always argue for a dual (or multiple) fulfillment of Isaish 13:19-20, but there are several considerations that limit the fulfillment of this prophecy to *ancient* Babylon.

First, Isaiah delivers oracles ("burdens" KJV) against Babylon and ten other groups that were enemies with Israel.[19] Why not take all these oracles as future prophecies yet to be fulfilled? They all speak of total destruction and devastation. The same hermeneutic principles must apply to all or none of these prophecies.

Second, notice that Isaiah predicted that Babylon would be overthrown by the Medes (Isaiah 13:17). This was fulfilled when the alliance of Medes and Persians took the city. To attempt to see the ancient Medes as the Kurds of Iraq, who oppose Hussein, seems a bit stretched and violates the original intention of the prophecy.

4. *The "Babylon" of the book of Revelation is symbolic of a future kingdom*

While the apostle John draws from Old Testament imagery, he clearly tells us that the Babylon of the future sits on "seven hills" and has ten kings (or kingdoms) within its borders (Revelation 17:9-12). Bible scholars are virtually unanimous in their agreement that John is talking about Rome in particular, and an extended European (or revised Roman) political system in the last days. This kingdom is so vast that it trades with the kings of the earth, carries an extensive variety of merchandise, is filled with musicians and craftsmen, is arrayed in great wealth, and is "drunken . . . with the blood of the martyrs of Jesus" (Revelation 17:6 KJV).

This prophetic "Babylon" is hardly modern-day Iraq! It is, rather, the epitome of a one-world Gentile government that will oppose God and His people in the last days. Rather than being a rebuilt Iraqi Babylon, the end-time Babylon is symbolic of all evil, pride, oppression, and power that exalts itself against God.[20] It will combine the best efforts of a collective humanity to rule itself without God. But it will fail!

Chapter 10

⊙⟆⟆⊙

GLOBALISM:
THE NEW WORLD ORDER

It was a far different world when Aldous Huxley wrote *Brave New World* in 1932. Yet the insightful Huxley saw ahead through the labyrinth of the future to a time when the World State would rise to power. In many ways, this volume was the most prophetic secular book of the twentieth century.

Instead of the Big Brother of George Orwell's *1984*, Huxley foresaw a world gone mad on materialism and pleasure-seeking to deaden its conscience against the value-emptied culture of high technology. His vision of human fertilization "farms" seemed absolutely unthinkable. Artificial insemination and genetic selection sounded like something out of a science fiction horror movie, but somehow Huxley knew the seeds of the future had already been sown in the past.

Huxley pictured people of the future as mindlessly pursuing an existence controlled by machines and soothed by pleasure. The past would become meaningless and intellectual, and the more noble pursuits of life would give way to the all-consuming pursuit of pleasure. One of the most intriguing dialogues in his book takes place between Fanny and Lenina, the one small-talking about the changes in society and the other small-talking about clothes, belts, shoes, and jewelry. The world of the future that Huxley foresaw was one that would readily sacrifice its principles for pleasure. It was a new world, unified politically and economically, whose god was itself—the World State.

President Bush talked frequently about the New Europe and the New World Order. In a live CNN broadcast on February 6, 1991, the president discussed the coming prosperity and stability of the New Europe in his address to the Economic Club of New York City. He seemed upbeat and hopeful when addressing this subject. There was a gleam in his eye as though he was touching upon something bigger than life.

The world is changing with breathtaking speed. John Naisbitt, the author of *Megatrends*,[1] says that the old ways of doing business and old styles of leadership are rapidly disappearing in an instant of macro change. He predicts a global economic boom for the 1990s. His projections are based on growing telecommunications capabilities and free trade among all nations. The United States, Europe, and Japan are the potential winners in the global bonanza. Even the global lifestyle will increase dramatically with extensive international travel, trade, and technological advances.

Prior to the Gulf War, the 1990s were being hailed as the most exciting and encouraging times in recent human history. "Never before has the prospect of world peace and prosperity seemed so promising," wrote one author before the invasion of Kuwait.[2] How quickly things changed when Operation Desert Shield was put into effect and then went into action as Operation Desert Storm!

THE PARTY'S OVER

Nineteen eighty-nine was the year of transformation in Eastern Europe. The walls of communism came crashing down so quickly that even the most ardent anticommunists were shocked. The whole world watched, stunned with near disbelief as the Iron Curtain was torn into shreds. More than 40 years had passed since Winston Churchill's famous speech at Westminster College in 1946, when he said, "An Iron Curtain has fallen across the continent."

The Iron Curtain mentality and the Cold War were harsh realities we all lived with in the years following World War II. They took the joy out of the Allied victory over Hitler's Germany because it left behind a divided world. Eastern Europe was dragged into the Soviet empire. In many ways the wars that followed in Korea and Vietnam were but ugly cancers that resulted from the failure to properly deal with the spoils of victory from World War II.

Then came the unexpected: Mikhail Gorbachev made it clear that the Soviet Union would no longer interfere in the internal policies of the Warsaw Pact nations of Eastern Europe. For nearly a decade prior to that announcement, people had been crying for democracy and freedom. The Solidarity movement had shaken Poland to the core. Though often criticized for doing so, evangelist Billy Graham preached in one communist country after another. He forged ahead believing God could make a difference behind the Iron Curtain, and he was right. The Christian revival in Romania exploded after Billy Graham's visit, and within weeks the communist dictatorship was overthrown.

Eastern-bloc countries began to open to other Christian leaders whose messages of life and hope in Christ brought a new wave of demand for religious freedom. Rev. Vernon Brewer, then vice president of Liberty University in Virginia, took hundreds of students behind the Iron Curtain in the 1980s to expose them to the future potential of evangelistic enterprise in Eastern Europe. Today the doors are wide open to Bibles, commentaries, missionaries, theological educators, and Christian workers. Brewer's World Help organization now ministers in virtually every nation in the former Soviet bloc.

EAST MEETS WEST

When Bush and Gorbachev met at Malta off the coast of Italy, *Time* magazine (December 11, 1989) flashed their smiling faces on the cover with the startling headline "Building a New World." Change was under way that would not be denied. In Gorbachev's meeting with Pope John Paul II, he said, "Having embarked upon the road of radical reform, the socialist countries are crossing the line beyond which there is no return to the past."[3]

While some people fear that these changes are part of a ploy to soften up the West, neutralize the United States, and undermine the NATO military alliance, it is clear that the cat is out of the bag! It is highly unlikely that the Soviets could regain control over their former satellite nations without long and serious military action against them.

The question facing the Russians now is whether they can even hold onto their own 15 republics. Independence movements have been aflame everywhere within the former Soviet Union—in Latvia, Estonia, Lithuania, Moldavia, and the six Muslim republics along the southern border. Dave Hunt observes, "One thing is certain: Much of Lenin's evil empire has gone up in flames, and the unlikely arsonist . . . was the Soviet president himself."[4]

A SEARCH FOR LEADERSHIP

The prospect of democracy, followed by capitalism, is sweeping across Eastern Europe, but it cannot survive without great difficulties. The emerging independence movement will likely fuel rising nationalism and could lead to the kind of conflicts that were going on in Europe prior to World War I. In one of these conflicts, ethnic enemies within Yugoslavia threatened to split the country apart.

Despite these challenges, the prospects for peace and economic cooperation are bright, but they probably won't come about unless there is some kind of strong personal leadership. George Bush saw himself in that kind of role. *Time* reported that Bush had resolved to "shape the new world order emerging in the aftermath of the Cold War."[5] At the same time, it is obvious that Gorbachev saw himself in that role as well. Now these leaders have been replaced by others. But the goals remain the same.

Public policy makers are now assuming that the new order will work only if the United States and Russia resolve to come together through the United Nations to provide a collective security for the future world. This theme certainly came through loud and clear in President Bush's televised address at the start of the offensive against Iraq. Twice in that speech he referred to the prospects of an internationally cooperative New World Order. Bush said, "We have before us the opportunity to forge for ourselves and for future generations a *New World Order.* . . . When we are successful, and we will be, we have a real chance at this *New World Order,* an order in which a credible UN can use its peace-keeping role to fulfill the promise and vision of the UN's founders"[6] (emphasis added).

THERE GOES THE NEIGHBORHOOD

In less than twelve months during 1989, the entire communist bloc of Eastern Europe overthrew its leadership and turned to democracy. The Hungarian parliament voted on January 11 to allow independent political parties. By May 2 Hungarian soldiers began cutting the barbed-wire fence, the literal Iron Curtain, along their country's border with Austria. On May 8 Hungary's communist dictator Janos Kadar was ousted from power, and by October 23 Hungary was an independent republic.

At the same time, the Roman Catholic Church and the Solidarity union joined hands to topple communism in Poland, with union leader Lech Walesa eventually being elected president. Then the other Eastern-bloc countries fell like a row of dominoes—Czechoslovakia, Bulgaria, and even Romania, where longtime communist dictator Nicolae Ceausescu was assassinated, all broke free from Moscow's control. Mikhail Gorbachev let it happen when he said the Soviets would make no attempt to intervene in Eastern Europe.

The Soviet Union (Russia and her 15 republics) and Albania stood alone as the last bastions of communism in Europe. Then came the stormy meeting on Malta between Bush and Gorbachev. There, on the same island where the apostle Paul was shipwrecked nearly 20 centuries ago (Acts 28:1-10), the two most powerful heads of state met to share a vision of a new world.

The earlier "summit" at Reykjavik, Iceland in 1986 opened with Gorbachev producing a list of sweeping arms proposals for Ronald Reagan. But at Malta it was Bush who produced a list of specific demands in the book-lined room on the Soviet cruise liner *Maxim Gorky*. As a winter storm pounded the vessel, the two leaders discussed the end of the Cold War. After sitting silent for most of Bush's hour-long presentation, Gorbachev said, "I have heard you say that you want *perestroika* to succeed, but frankly, I didn't know this. Now I know."[7]

A NEW WORLD ORDER?

When Gorbachev and Bush began talking about a "new world order," evangelical Christians sat up and took careful notice.[8] "What do they mean?" people asked one another. Are they talking about a post-Cold War world with increased global technology and peaceful international cooperation, or are they talking about the political, economic, and even religious union that the Scripture warns against in the last days?

To the secular press the new order sounded like good news. Finally, the two world heavyweights were going to take off their boxing gloves and try to shake hands. Certainly, Christians and non-Christians alike should rejoice over the thaw in the Cold War and desire that peace be given a chance.

But biblically perceptive Christians also know that this last attempt at peace is tentative and temporary at best. It is the height of naivete to think that depraved, sinful human beings can solve their own conflicts apart from God.

All previous attempts at structuring a world order have, without fail, fallen on the harsh realities of man's pride, arrogance, greed, avarice, and self-destruction. Woodrow Wilson's League of Nations failed to stop World War II, and the present United Nations has struggled since its very inception. Yet there seems to be something within the international community propelling us toward a unified world system. Many fear that driving force is Satan himself.

THE ROMAN CONNECTION

En route to Malta, Gorbachev stopped at Rome for the first-ever meeting of a Soviet leader with a pope. It was a momentous occasion and may have marked the beginning of some kind of reconciliation between the atheistic Soviet Union and the Roman Catholic and Russian Orthodox churches. It was another of those shocking events that hit so quickly and unexpectedly that we could hardly believe it. The leader of a party and nation formally committed to atheism was calling Pope John Paul II "your holiness" as they conferred for 75 minutes in the library of the sixteenth-century Apostolic Palace at the Vatican.

"We need spiritual values," Gorbachev had declared the day before in his remarks in Rome's city hall, where the Treaty of Rome, establishing the European Community, had been signed in 1957.[9] Everything seemed so well programmed that one might wonder if Satan himself were calling the shots.

In his meeting with the pope, Gorbachev promised greater religious freedom and talked about spiritual values. While the secular media thought all that was good news, evangelical Christians became concerned about a political, economic, and social alliance of Europe with the heads of formal religion.

"Doesn't the Bible warn us against both a political and religious Antichrist in the last days?" a friend asked me at the time.

The book of Revelation predicts the coming of a beast with ten horns and seven heads (Revelation 13:1), which embodies the characteristics of Daniel's prophecy of the empires of the lion, bear, and leopard (Daniel 7). In other words, this coming world power will be the personification and embodiment of the whole history of world powers.[10] It will also be empowered by Satan—"the dragon" himself (Revelation 13:2). Whoever or whatever this "beast coming out of the sea" (Revelation 13:1) is, he openly blasphemes God and makes war on the saints of God. Yet "all inhabitants of the earth will worship the beast" (Revelation 13:8).

The book of Revelation also points to "another beast, coming out of the earth" who looks like a lamb but talks like a dragon (Revelation 13:11). What is unique about the second Beast is that he is able to get all the inhabitants of the earth to "worship the first beast" (Revelation 13:12). He deceives the inhabitants of earth and causes them to worship the "image of the first beast" (Revelation 13:15) and to receive his mark, so that "no one could buy or sell unless he had the mark, which is the name of the beast or the number of his name" (Revelation 13:17).

Clearly, this prophecy speaks of the religious, political, and economic control of the world at the end of the age by a combination of political and religious powers. The book of Revelation also depicts this power as "the great prostitute" (Revelation 17:1ff). She too is associated with the Beast's seven heads and ten horns (Revelation 17:3). Since the time of the Reformation in the sixteenth century, many Protestants have identified this woman as the Catholic Church in Rome. The prophecy itself says, "The seven heads are seven hills on which the woman sits" (Revelation 17:9). The ten horns are "ten kings who have *not yet* received a kingdom" (Revelation 17:12, emphasis added) but will do so in connection with the Beast. Thus, they are clearly predicted as something yet to come in the future.

A New Reformation?

In a powerful and insightful editorial in *Newsweek* magazine, political commentator George Will compared the startling changes that are taking place in Europe to the Reformation of the sixteenth century.

> It is just 60 miles from Berlin to Wittenberg, where the 34-year-old Luther nailed his 95 theses to the church door. Four years later at the Diet of Worms he spoke [the] words that define the modern frame of mind . . . "Here I stand, I can do no other." The primary idea of the Reformation was the primacy of individual conscience. It has been the high-octane fuel of all subsequent history.[11]

In Will's assessment, the greatest failure of communism was its ideological assault on individualism. Socialism had impoverished every facet of individual life. People were eager for a change, and as soon as freedom from socialism became even a remote possibility they ignited a spontaneous grassroots revolt that swept quickly across Eastern Europe and knocked down the obstacles to democracy.

Project 1992

"Europhoria," a mood of exuberance, is sweeping Europe these days. Ideological barriers are falling everywhere, borders are blurring, and the continent is coming together. The "chunnel" (tunnel) under the English Channel, completed in 1990, made it possible to drive from Paris to London in a few hours. That marked the first time in history that England has been land-connected to the rest of Europe. So not only the governments and politics of Europe are changing, but even the geographics.

Europe had a banner year in 1992 when Spain hosted both the Summer Olympics and the World's Fair. But the real excitement was the economic integration of Western Europe in 1992. The longtime dream of European unity became a reality by December 31, 1992, when the 12 members of the European Economic Community (EEC) united their economic markets to create the largest trading bloc and free market economy in the world.

Time magazine declared, "Project 1992 has given fresh momentum . . . to taking Western Europe further down the road to unity."[12] With the collapse of communism in Eastern Europe, the prospect for an all-united Europe may finally become a reality in the not too distant future. Several leaders are involved in a project called the "Continental Express," and France's Jacques Delors has been the chief engineer behind creating a united Europe since becoming president of the European Commission in 1985. He was personally responsible for setting 1992 as the target date to make it all happen.

Delors has called for a unified currency for all of Europe, common European passports, and even the possibility of political unification—all in the name of material prosperity and success. "We must build Europe every day," he has said. "We must go all the way."[13] His tenacity drove Margaret Thatcher out of office and even forced French Socialist Francois Mitterand to get in step with the project.

It is no wonder Delors has earned the nickname "Mr. Europe." *U.S. News & World Report* predicted a unified Western Europe by 1995, adding, "Less passionate crusaders than Jacques Delors are squinting at the year 2000—and holding their breath."[14] Whatever the pace or the obstacles ahead, the idea is alive and well. Britain's Prime Minister, John Major, is one of its strongest advocates. In December 1990 the European Commission approved major steps designed to propel the EEC beyond economic boundaries toward real political union in the future. The goal is for the European Economic Community (EEC) to become the European Community (EC). A light-blue flag with a circle of 12 stars has already been prepared.

WHY ALL THE EXCITEMENT?

Megatrends 2000 addressed the question of what 1992 was all about with a concise and practical list:[15]

- 1992 means that a Greek lawyer will be able to set up a practice in Copenhagen and that a Spanish shoe company could open a shop unhindered in Dublin.
- 1992 means that a Japanese or American businessman can fly into one European Community country, pass through customs once, and then visit the other eleven without seeing another customs or immigration official.
- 1992 means that a Portuguese bank can be the partner of a new venture in the Paris fashion industry.
- 1992 means goods and people moving as easily from France to Germany as they can from California to Oregon.
- 1992 means that there will be more competition at all levels of the single market, bringing greater choice of attractively priced goods and services.

HOW WILL IT WORK?

The philosophy behind the dream is fairly simple: forge Europe into one cohesive market in order to compete with the United States and Japan on a global scale. Three things must occur before this can happen, and all the rest will fall in place.

First, *physical* barriers, such as customs posts, frontier controls, and product restrictions, must be removed. This will eliminate long lines and mountains of paperwork at the borders of each member country.

Second, *technical* barriers involving different standards and regulations to which businesses have to comply will be unified. Any goods or services lawfully produced in one member country can automatically be marketed in another.

Third, *fiscal* barriers, such as luxury taxes, and food, wine, and hotel taxes, which vary greatly from one country to another, will be standardized. The result will bring "a dramatic change in the world of European retailing," states Eric Salama of the Henley Centre for Forecasting in London.[16] This will also improve retailers' ability to obtain products from all the member countries of the European Economic Community.

However, Salama warns, consumer tastes vary enormously across Europe and not all goods will sell as well in every member nation. Old habits, culture, and language barriers will still remain. In general, however, the big goal of unifying the internal market, proposed when the Treaty of Rome was signed in 1957, was finally realized in 1992.

The original treaty envisioned *both* an economic and political unification of Europe before the end of the twentieth century. The passing of the Single European Act by the members of the EEC now makes that dream a potential reality in the near future. International Banker Nicholas Colchester states, "The agreement to lift national controls on the flow of capital is, in my view, the most striking concession to the idea of a single market so far made."[17]

THE POWER OF THE COMPUTER

The real key to making the New Europe work will be the personal computer. "Computer power," writes John Lamb, editor of *Computer Weekly*, "is now at the executive's fingertips . . . linking computers, large and small, to a central clearing house."[18] The computer spreadsheet will replace the pocket calculator as financial transactions in the New Europe leap across computer screens from businesses to banks to manufacturers to retailers and even into private homes all across the continent.

Such high-speed computer networks all across Europe will bring the continent together economically and eventually politically in a way that no military action ever could. The political integration of Europe will ride on the shoulders of computer integration.

The impersonal computer screen will carry visual images, by means of scanners that "turn pictures into a digital form suitable for processing and able to be displayed on a computer screen."[19] All of this information will be stored and processed in a gigantic computer at the EEC's central headquarters in Brussels, Belgium. Some have actually called the monstrous computer "the Beast." Eventually it will be used to control all of Europe's economic transactions.

Christians, of course, are concerned about where all this might lead. There is certainly nothing wrong with computers and electronic imagery and cashless financial transactions. The big problem is that it all becomes one more giant step for impersonal technology. We are already prisoners of our own technology and will likely become more enslaved by it. Electric windows in an automobile are great until they refuse to open on a hot day and you are left sweltering in a closed-up automobile. Technology itself is neither moral nor immoral. The ultimate issue is *how* we use that technology or how *it* uses us.

A Modern Tower of Babel?

The official poster of the Council of Europe depicts the European Community as the Tower of Babel under construction, with twelve stars representing the twelve nations of the New Europe. The hope of the future is captured in the caption: "Europe: Many Tongues, One Voice."

An evangelical writer noticed that the European edition of the *Wall Street Journal,* for the second quarter of 1990, contained an insert from IBM that also depicted the New Europe as the Tower of Babel.[20] This may be a mere coincidence, but it does make us wonder: Bible prophecy predicts the rise of a symbolic "Babylon" that will control the economic and political world of the last days. Is this beginning to happen before our very eyes?

The Roman Empire Revisited

Daniel's prophecy of the final world empire, with two legs and two feet with ten toes (Daniel 2), generally has been interpreted as Byzantine Rome (east and west) and an eventual revived Rome (or Europe) of the last days. The two legs symbolize the two halves of the Roman Empire since Constantine moved the capital to Byzantium (Constantinople).

The eastern part of the Roman Empire reached from Constantinople northward into the fringes of Russia, eastward through the Middle East, and south toward Egypt and North Africa. The primary language in the Eastern Empire was Greek, and the predominant religion was the Eastern Orthodox church. Their missionary enterprise took Christianity to Russia and the Ukraine in the tenth and eleventh centuries. For this reason the Russian Orthodox Church and the Russian language, which is written in a Greek-influenced alphabet, owe much to the eastern wing of the old Roman Empire.

The western part of the Roman Empire covered most of continental Europe and extended all the way to Great Britain. In the west, Latin was the predominant language and the Roman Catholic Church was the primary religion. British Christianity and, in turn, American Christianity were influenced more by this wing of the empire. For example, American churches usually follow the Catholic dates for Christmas and Easter, rather than the Orthodox dates.

As we've seen throughout this book, many people believe that the New Europe of the future may well be an economically and politically united Europe encompassing much of the old Roman Empire. The Rome Treaty itself even suggests Rome as a possible capital for a unified government. This, however, does not mean that the common market is necessarily all bad, or that Christians ought to refuse to have anything to do with technological advance that might be used by the government of the New Europe—advances such as computers and bar codes. But the world could be marching in concert to a drummer it doesn't even know is there—Satan himself.

HERE COMES THE BEAST

The Bible depicts the Antichrist as the "beast coming out of the sea" whose "fatal wound had been healed" (Revelation 13:1,3). Some people believe this wound refers to the assassination of some great leader who rises in Europe in the last days or to the recovery of the corpse of the old Roman Empire aided by false religion, the False Prophet.

The interpretation of who these figures are hinges on whether they are individuals or collective entities or both. In Revelation 19:20 we read that someday the Beast and the False Prophet will be cast into the lake of fire; that passage seems to indicate two persons—two separate individuals. But the words about the seven hills and ten horns seem to symbolize a political system. In light of these clues, perhaps it is best to see the Beast as both a leader and a system which he controls.

The apostle John said that the spirit of false teaching, already active in the first century, was a form of the spirit of Antichrist. He wrote, "This is the spirit of the antichrist, which you have heard is coming and even now is already in the world" (1 John 4:3). In the broadest sense, the Antichrist is already here. The book of Revelation tells us that Satan is the real power behind him, and Satan has been around for a very long time.

It would seem to me that we must reconcile these various elements of prophecy by recognizing: 1) that the spirit of Antichrist (Satan) is already operating in the world; 2) there will come a political, material, economic, and religious world system in the last days which is in itself "antichrist"; 3) there will emerge a powerful individual who will control that system and use it for evil against God's people.

By allowing the full fruition of these prophecies to touch every possible aspect of this future evil enterprise, we can let the *facts* of prophecy stand clear from our limitied *assumptions* and *speculations*.

A MATTER OF TIMING

The ultimate problem with prophecies about the end times

is that it's very difficult to determine how close our present age is to those days. It has been a common error throughout church history for Christians to *assume* they were living in the last days. When a person accepts his own day as the end times, he can speculate that any contemporary event may be a fulfillment of prophecy. But if his timing is off, then the *speculation* will collapse.

The global trends emerging today point to the *possibility* of changes necessary for the events of end-times prophecy to unfold. But this does not prove they will develop the way we think they will. For example, the grand experiment of the European Community could fail disastrously and come to naught. The Soviet Union may or may not continue toward democracy. It may or may not move closer to the New Europe. There is no way to know what will happen without speculating.

Christ may return today or He may not come for another 200 years. But we *can* be certain about the following matters because the *facts* of prophecy say so:

- Wars, conflicts, and natural disasters will continue through the present age (Matthew 24:6-7).
- The gospel must continue to be preached until Christ returns (Matthew 24:14).
- False prophets will deceive many people throughout the present age (Matthew 24:24).
- No one knows the date of Christ's return (Matthew 24:36).
- Believers are to remain faithful in their service to Christ and be ready for Him to come at any time (Matthew 24:42-51).
- "Terrible times" will come in the last days, signified by a rebellious and indulgent society (2 Timothy 3:1-5).
- A great deceiver will arise in the last days and lead the world astray (2 Thessalonians 2:1-12).
- The church will be "caught up" in the rapture when Christ comes for His own (1 Thessalonians 4:13-18).

- A time of Great Tribulation will burst upon the world as a result of God's judgment against sin (Revelation 6-19).
- Jesus Christ will come at the end of the Tribulation at the Battle of Armageddon to overthrow the unholy trinity: Satan, Antichrist, and the False Prophet (Revelation 19:11-21).
- Christ shall rule on earth for 1,000 years in His millennial reign (Revelation 20:1-6).
- Satan, death, and hell will all be cast into the lake of fire after the Millennium (Revelation 20:10-15) and the new heavens and new earth will usher in the eternal kingdom (Revelation 21–22).

This is the coming new world order that will last forever. It is not the device or plan of men; it is the eternal kingdom of God, which reigns over all the universe, from eternity to eternity. To this we say, "Come quickly, Lord Jesus!"

Chapter 11

⟨∞∞⟩

WHAT IS AHEAD FOR THE 21ST CENTURY?

When I was a boy, talk about the twenty-first century was usually limited to the realm of science fiction, but now the twenty-first century is very real and right at hand. We are now entering the third millennium of church history. Just as the twentieth century marked a dramatic change from the past, so will the twenty-first century mark an even more dramatic change for the future.

We are now on the verge of the most dynamic century in world history. Computer technology and satellite communication have made it possible for every corner of the world to become interconnected to a massive global network that could well set the stage for the final days of earth's history.

The very number *2000* has an ominous ring to it. While it is only a date on a man-made calendar, it does remind us that we are moving ahead into uncharted waters.

John Naisbitt and Patricia Aburdene, authors of *Megatrends 2000,* have observed:

Already we have fallen under its dominion. The

> year 2000 is operating like a powerful magnet on humanity, reaching down into the 1990s and intensifying the decade. It is amplifying emotions, accelerating change, heightening awareness, and compelling us to reexamine ourselves, our values, and our institutions.[1]

Visions of the future are generally optimistic or pessimistic. Some people see great hope on the horizon. They are quick to remind us that the Cold War is over, militarism is out, and the economy is about to boom. By contrast, other people fear that we are racing headlong toward destruction. They remind us that the economy is struggling, the environment is deteriorating, and the world is still a political time bomb that could go off at any moment.

I believe that *both* visions of the future are true. Call it a boom-and-doom mentality if you like, but that is exactly what I see. We are at a great crossroads in human history. We could go either way. The choice will be up to us. If we make the right choices, the days ahead could be the greatest ever. But if we make the wrong choices, the consequences will be disastrous.

MILLENNIAL MILESTONES

Big numbers tend to get our attention: *2000* is such a number. It will hit like a lightning bolt when it arrives. People will hardly be able to imagine writing the date in their checkbooks. Calendars will look strange to us at first. Our years will begin with the number 2.

Once we fully realize the impact of a new millennium, we will begin to ask ourselves what we are really all about. Self-evaluation will cause many people to stop and reflect on the real meaning and value of life. But unless that reflection drives us to biblical answers, our problems will only grow more enormous than ever.

Russell Chandler, religion editor for *The Los Angeles Times,* observes that a speed-of-light cultural revolution is already under way. In his compelling new book *Racing Toward 2001*, Chandler looks at the forces shaping America's religious future.[2] He warns that we must be aware of both the wonders of technology and its inherent potential for the subversion of our spiritual values.

Chandler notes that "information-hungry technology in a high-surveillance society can erode our freedoms and compromise our privacy."[3] Information about the average American is stored in 18 federal computers, 16 state and local computers, and 25 private computers. While all of this creates a climate of accountability, it also creates a potential "Big Brother" who is always watching.

The combination of *photonics* and *fiber optics* makes it possible for a single strand of fiber to transmit 16,000 telephone calls at once at a speed so fast the entire text of the Bible could be transmitted in less than two seconds. Chandler observes that the photonic systems, wedded to high-tech electronics, are "combining these functions with higher speed, smaller size, lower power, and less cost than ever before."[4]

The great danger of the technological revolution is that it is void of spiritual values. Chandler warns, "If worshipped, technology in the end proves to be a false god, corroding human values and desensitizing the spirit."[5] The spiritual emptiness of our culture will leave it vulnerable to the great deception of the last days.

THE REAL AND THE IMAGINARY

The power of video imagery is so great that it is often difficult for us to distinguish between the real and the imagined. After thousands of hours of television, most Americans aren't sure what they have seen or what it really means. In his insightful critique of the "Age of Show Business," Neil Postman writes in the book *Amusing Ourselves to Death* that we have descended into a "vast triviality."[6]

Postman sees Americans as mindless individuals constantly seeking to be entertained. The ascendancy of the age of television thrusts us into what he calls a dramatic and irreversible shift in the content and meaning of public discourse: The medium (television) becomes the message.

Because video imagery is so prominent in our culture, it is difficult for many Americans to deal with reality. Some people are reluctant to help those who are being assaulted, robbed, or raped, simply because they can't believe it is happening before their eyes. "It all seemed like I was watching a movie," explained one college-aged bystander.

Ernst Cassirer has observed that "physical reality seems to recede in proportion as man's symbolic activity advances."[7] Thus, the medium of televised images becomes our reality. We actually believe what we see and act accordingly. Just as the invention of the clock turned people into timekeepers, then timesavers, and now time-servants, so television has turned us from television-watchers to television-slaves.

Thus, there is real power in televised images. I say this with respect, having been on television myself for so many years, but it is true! Whether I am awake or asleep at a given moment does not affect how a viewer perceives me during a video replay. As far as the viewer is concerned, I am talking to him or her at that moment. While this has great technological advantages, it is also fraught with problems.

Televised images make us believe that Indiana Jones can fall off a truck, be dragged behind it for a long time, and still have enough strength to overpower the driver, climb a mountain, fly an airplane, and not be out of energy. But in reality, that's not humanly possible. Therefore, the danger of television or movies is that we create an artificial sense of reality.

It is quite possible this is what Bible prophecy warns against when it talks about the "image" of the Beast (Revelation 13:15). Holographic images, which are three-dimensional and lifelike in every detail are already a reality. We are constantly bombarded with technological imagery that shapes the ideas and beliefs of our society. There is no doubt in my mind that the final deception has already begun.

TECHNOLOGICAL ADVANCES

Lest anyone think this trend will turn around, think again. The explosion of the information age is already upon us. In the years ahead, our knowledge base will be greatly expanded, memory storage capabilities will be dramatically increased, and information will be available to us faster and easier than ever before. Our lives will be shaped by global technology networks.

The future will likely include electronic (or "smart") houses fully equipped with voice-activated computers and work-at-home offices. The computer-literate generations of the future will be even more likely to adapt quickly and uncritically to technological changes. People will be able to simulate reality so they can escape reality. Homes of the future will be equipped with high-definition television, surround-sound systems, and giant wall screens that can deliver simulated reality in total-experience chambers.

Robots will also be a part of the new millennium. They will be used to perform basic services or dangerous tasks—such as entering a burning building to rescue survivors. Already, today's "smart weapons" use electronic sensors and computer brains to pinpoint and destroy enemies. Their use during the Gulf War was highly profiled in the newscasts.

Artificial intelligence and artificial life could become realities in the world ahead. This will only further blur the lines between the real world and the artificial one. It will also raise a flood of questions about the ethics of "playing God." Reproductive experimentation, fetal tissue transplants, and genetic engineering will place man in the role of God, giving him the capability to determine who will be born, what their quality of life should be, and which people will be left out.

The ethical questions people ask will slow the progress of the information explosion, but they will not stop it. Despite human concerns, the "spirit of the age" will carry us on to a technologically advanced future.

WHERE ARE WE GOING?

With the advancement of modernity has come a restless uneasiness about the traditional values that are slipping away from our society.[8] We seem to be discarding the very values and concepts that made America great. God has been gradually and systematically removed from public life. Prayer and Bible reading have been forbidden in the public schools.

In the place of God, our public schools are filled with violence, crime, alcohol, and drugs. Our cities have turned away from God only to become infested with the worst kinds of crime. People, in general, have turned to mysticism and the occult to find meaning and purpose in their lives.

Ours has been called an age of selfism. The self-centered pursuit of self-gratification has dominated modern life in the past 20 years. We have become a society hung up on itself—a society without leaders. Everyone is caught up in making it big for himself, and most people aren't interested in the common good of others. Allan Bloom writes, "Country, religion, family, ideas of civilization, all the sentimental and historical forces that stood between cosmic infinity and the individual . . . have been rationalized away and have lost their compelling force."[9]

This moral vacuum leaves society to its own devices. *Self*-interest, *self*-appeasement, and *self*-gratification have become the motivating factors in our public and private lives. The great danger of all this selfism is that it paves the way for the appeasement of evil in our society. The abandonment of moral absolutes is justified on the basis that such absolutes conflict with *our* lives, *our* freedoms, and *our* choices. But without a biblical standard (or any absolutes), we have no guideline to judge actions as morally right or wrong. Therefore, it should not surprise us that our secularized society is willing to tolerate abortion, euthanasia, and even infanticide.

A NATION WITHOUT GOD

Francis Schaeffer said that the church's accommodation to the spirit of the age would lead to "the removal of the last barrier against the breakdown of our culture."[10] Former Surgeon General C. Everett Koop calls this indifference to moral issues the "slide to Auschwitz."[11] Once the philosophers, theologians, and medical personnel abandon moral absolutes, the door to human atrocities has already opened.

Godless humanism is sweeping America with its blatant rejection of moral absolutes and traditional values. It has sought to secularize virtually every aspect of American life—leaving God and the Bible totally outside the parameters of relevance. Death by neglect is their strategy. Humanists think that if they can get everyone to stop talking about God, He will simply go away. "Stop publicizing His existence and people will forget about God," one humanist recently stated.

R.C. Sproul defines humanism as an anthropocentric (man-centered) view of life as opposed to a theocentric (God-centered) view of life.[12] To the humanist, man, not God, is the ultimate measure of all things. Humanists reject the ideas of a divine being and divinely revealed moral absolutes.

The unique problem of the late twentieth century is that modern technology can translate the humanist message into television, films, and videos almost instantly. These entertaining mediums can then communicate a non-Christian or even anti-Christian message that is often received uncritically by the viewer/listener.

Bible teacher John MacArthur observed, "Humanism and secularism . . . are eroding the foundations of the Christian faith."[13] He notes that these influences are more dangerous than the liberalization that assaulted the church in the early twentieth century. Modern humanism is more subtle and less detectible to the average person. It is spreading even in the church with alarming effectiveness.

Ironically, modern man has come to the conclusion that he needs hope beyond himself, but he is looking for it in all the wrong places. Mysticism, collective consciousness, and channelling have replaced devotion, prayer, and Scripture. People are trying to find God via experiences instead of bowing in submission to the God of the Bible.

CHURCHES AND THE GLOBAL SOCIETY

Society is a collection of individuals, and the global society is a global collection of individuals. Prospects for the twenty-first century will reveal the demise of collectivism, already heralded by the collapse of communism and the rise of individualism. Many people see today's technology as empowering the individual, who can work at home with a computer, modem, and fax machine and network with the entire global system. That will make the new technology appealing at first, but it will also entrap those who become dependent on it.

John Naisbitt foresees a new "Electronic Heartland" of information processors who can live anywhere they choose, "linked by telephones, fax machines, Federal Express, and computers."[14] He predicts this will affect population demographics in the years ahead. In 1990 he noted that the 14 million full-time, home-based businesses in America would jump to 20 million by 1995.

Naisbitt also sees the need for a genuine religious revival that emphasizes the individuality of faith and a transcendent experience with God. Old, traditional religious patterns will be challenged by nontraditional worship and educational innovations. Dr. Elmer Towns, dean of the School of Religion at Liberty University, has observed these trends about today's innovative churches:[15]

1. Geographically expanded parishes
2. Local identity with shared management
3. Satellite churches or services
4. Innovative worship/music/teaching
5. Multiple ministries led by laymen
6. Cell groups or affinity groups
7. Specifically targeted evangelism

Church growth expert George Barna has observed that the ministries that succeed in the future will be those that do a few things well rather than those that try to be all things to all people. "Each church has been called to uniqueness and ought to explore ways of exploiting its uniqueness in service to God," Barna reports.[16]

THE CHANGES IN FAMILY LIFE

The traditional family has been under assault now for nearly three decades. The sexual revolution of the 1960s has left the fractured remains of broken homes and shattered marriages all across the American landscape. And with one million divorces each year since 1975, it is not likely we will ever see the family unit of the past as the stabilizing force in the society of the future.

In 1960, married couples made up 75 percent of U.S. households. Today they represent about 45 percent. There are now 3 million households headed up by unmarried couples. That represents an 80 percent increase since 1980. In 1995, one of every eight children was born out of wedlock.

Redefining the Family

Russell Chandler points out these characteristics of today's families:[17]

- By 2000, more than 50 percent of all children will spend part of their lives in single-parent homes.
- By 2010, one-third of all American families will be "blended" families because of divorce and remarriage.
- Most mothers will be working mothers for most of their adult lives.
- Interracial marriage will change the look of the American family of the future.
- There will be increasing pressure to redefine "family" in nontraditional terms.

Dual-career parents, single-parent families, unmarried couples, and blended families are not just future issues facing the family. These arrangements exist in many families today. The struggle to balance work and home life is a problem for most couples. Quality time at home is something we all claim we want, but very few parents succeed at providing it. Child-care and day-care centers provide a kind of surrogate parenting, but many parents wonder if instead they should be at home with their children.

Recent studies revealed that the second-income spouse (usually, though not always, the wife) loses nearly 75 percent of his or her income to increased child care costs; car, travel, dress, and lunch expenses; and increased taxes. Many second-income earners would do well to ask themselves whether it is really worthwhile to work outside the home. Of course, some people say they must work to survive financially, yet there are others who want to work only for their own personal and professional fulfillment.

The Impact of Divorce

Single-parent families are another reality that must be faced in our modern age. Thirty-three percent of all single-parent homes are headed by a divorced mother; 28 percent by a never-married mother; and 22 percent by a separated mother.[18] The breakup of marriages is one of the great tragedies of our time. But it is also a fact of life. The church of the future *must* be willing to minister to single parents and divorced people who are in need. Otherwise we will miss an entire segment of the population who needs the gospel of God's grace and forgiveness. These people also need Christian friendship and nurturing from a body of believers who truly care about them and their needs.

The increased number of divorces and remarriages will, in turn, increase the number of blended families in America. The Step-family Association of America estimates that there are now 35 million step-parents in America with 1,300 new step-families formed every day. Like it or not, we must be ready to provide the counseling, classes, and family services to meet these growing needs while doing all we can to stem the tide of divorce.

People used to try to excuse divorce by asserting that it didn't hurt the children involved. "Kids are resilient; they'll bounce back!" I have often heard people say. But recent psychological studies do *not* confirm that at all! Rather, these studies show that divorce has a devastating effect on children.[19] Many adult children of divorce cannot overcome their fears of rejection or make lasting commitments themselves.

I believe the church must minister actively to married people and help them remain committed to marriage. But the church must also minister to separated and divorced people as well. That's the only way we are going to reach the next generation in our world.

THE FUTURE OF EDUCATION

The future of public education in America is bleak. Test scores are down, educators are discouraged, and classroom discipline is in a serious crisis. The high school dropout rate is higher than ever for blacks and Hispanics. Gang wars plague most big-city schools. High degrees of functional illiteracy affect about half of all high-school graduates. Many young people today can't read or write, and what's worse is that they don't care!

The ultimate crisis in education is spiritual and philosophical. Public universities sold their souls to secularism early in this century and have survived to reap the consequences. The void of spiritual values has led to the great ethical crises of our times. People just don't care what is right or wrong anymore. All they care about is themselves. Mark Schwehn of Valparaiso University observed, "The modern university has forgotten its spiritual foundations."[20]

In the meantime, Dorothy Bass of the University of Chicago has observed this same trend in many church-related colleges as well. "It's hard to know a church-affiliated college when you see one," she says.[21] This tragic drift toward secularism has already taken place in many schools that were originally founded on spiritual principles. It is the nature of the academic beast to wander to the left and away from its roots unless strong minds and hands keep it on track with its original mission statement and purpose.

James Davidson Hunter of the University of Virginia has warned that the coming generation of evangelical Christians may be in danger of drifting away from the fundamental beliefs that once defined evangelicalism.[22] While this possibility certainly exists, it underscores the importance of Christian educators emphasizing the Christian distinctives in their schools and institutions.

When we look at the trends of our times and the biblical prophecies of the end times, we see more and more that we may be running out of time to reach our generation for Christ. We cannot wait for somebody else to do the job. We must act now to reach the people around us. We can do it and we must do it . . . while there is still time!

Chapter 12

❦

WHERE DO WE GO FROM HERE?

Ever since the Tower of Babel (Genesis 11), mankind has seemed determined to rally its collective forces together in defiance of God. That's not to say that cooperation itself is bad, but there seems to be something about the pride of unregenerate men that tells them they can make it without God. It is as though people think that if enough of them band together, they can make almost anything happen.

I believe we are now moving in that direction. The years ahead are pointing toward a greater international network than mankind has ever known. Left unchecked, it will evolve into a powerful political, economic, and military machine. Headquartered in Europe, it will represent the political revival of the Roman Empire.

The stage is now set for the fulfillment of end-times Bible prophecies. Israel is back in her land after a 2,000-year absence. The New Europe is coming together on the continent after sixteen centuries of division. The United States, the most powerful nation in the world, seems ready to join forces with the new global community.

The timing of the last days is up to God. But from a human standpoint, it would appear that we are standing on the threshold of the final frontier. I don't think the pieces of the puzzle could be in place any better than they are right now.

BALANCING THE TENSION

Each of us must plan our lives as though we will live for many more years to come. We have a responsibility to our families, children, grandchildren, and other people around us. But we must also live our lives as though Jesus could come at any moment. It is difficult for non-Christians to understand the balanced approach we must have toward the future. We Christians do not fear the future because we believe God controls it. But at the same time, we do not view it with unbridled optimism.

The tension between living for today and looking forward to tomorrow is one of the realities of life. Christians especially find themselves caught in that tension between the here and now and the hereafter. Though we are enjoying our daily walk of faith here on earth, we also have a desire to depart and be with Christ. The apostle Paul spoke about this tension when he wrote "For to me, to live is Christ and to die is gain" (Philippians 1:21).

Bible prophecy emphasizes that we need to be ready because Christ could come at any time. Because of the imminence of His return, we must be waiting and watching every moment. At the same time, we have serious responsibilities to fulfill in this world. We cannot use our belief in Christ's return as an excuse to avoid our responsibilities.

The Bible not only tells us how to prepare for the future, but it also tells us how to live right now. It tells us about the future destiny of the nations, but it also speaks about our personal destiny as well. As the sands of time slip through the hourglass of eternity, we are all moving closer to an appointment with God in the future.

Once you settle the question of your eternal destiny, you can better determine the present course of your life. Your choices and values will be determined by eternity. No longer will your decisions be made in light of their immediate consequences; rather, they will be made in light of their eternal significance.

THE BLESSED HOPE

The Bible refers to Christ's return as the "blessed hope—the glorious appearing of our great God and Savior, Jesus Christ" (Titus 2:13). The sheer joy of knowing that one day we will be raptured into the presence of Christ causes all earthly concerns to fade into oblivion. It is no wonder the Bible reminds us: "Our citizenship is in heaven. And we eagerly await a Savior from there, the Lord Jesus Christ" (Philippians 3:20).

Dave Hunt notes that a person cannot look for the coming of Christ at any moment if he believes Jesus will not return until after the tribulation period. Hunt observes, "If the rapture could not occur until after the Antichrist has first appeared, or until the end of the great tribulation, surely such language would not have been used."[1] He goes on to point out that the imminent return of Christ was the daily hope of the early Christians.

Rather than possessing an escapist mentality, prophecy students have an earnest desire to be ready at all times to meet the Lord, who could come at any moment to call us home. We want to be watching, ready, and serving. That's what our Lord commanded in the Olivet Discourse (see Matthew 24:42-46).

A readiness to meet the Lord when He returns is one of the great motivations of the Christian life. First, we must be certain that we know Christ as our Savior. Second, we must live out our faith by being ready to meet Him at any moment. Dave Hunt writes, "That is the Christian's hope. Heaven is our real home and that is where our hearts are—with Him."[2]

Nature Waits in Anticipation

The only real hope for planet earth is the return of Christ. Ecologists, naturalists, and conservationists will never save this planet. New Age politicians with global aspirations will not save this globe. Antinuclear demonstrators will not save the earth. The Bible tells us that "the creation waits in eager expectation for the sons of God to be revealed" when Jesus Christ returns (Romans 8:19).

When Jesus returns with His raptured church, the deterioration of the planet will cease. The devastation that resulted from the wars of the tribulation period will be reversed. The earth will blossom under the peaceful rule of the Prince of Peace. But without Christ on the throne, this planet is headed for serious trouble. Only He can overrule the degradation of sin, the destruction of war, and the devastation of the planet.

What We Can Expect

Speculating about the future beyond what the Bible itself predicts is a dangerous game. Psychics make hundreds of predictions every year that never come true. But a gullible general public doesn't seem to care. They quickly run out to buy the next list of predictions for next year. Bible prophecy, however, does not work that way. The prophets sent by God made many predictions about the first and second comings of Christ thousands of years ago. Their prophecies have stood the test of time; many have been fulfilled and there are more prophecies about certain future events that are inevitable:

- The spread of the gospel and the *growth of the church* through the worldwide evangelism of all nations (Matthew 24:14).
- The rise of *religious apostasy* in the last days, leading to widespread sin and lawlessness (2 Thessalonians 2:3).
- The *rapture of the church* (true believers) to heaven

MAJOR EVENTS OF UNFULFILLED PROPHECY

ᥤᴥᴥᨆ ᥤᴥᴥᨆ ᥤᴥᴥᨆ

1. Rapture of the church (1 Corinthians 15:51-58; 1 Thessalonians 4:13-18)
2. Revival of the Roman Empire; ten-nation confederacy formed (Daniel 7:7,24; Revelation 13:1; 17:3; 12-13)
3. Rise of the Antichrist: the Middle East dictator (Daniel 7:8; Revelation 13:18)
4. The seven-year peace treaty with Israel: consummated seven years before the second coming of Christ (Daniel 9:27; Revelation 13:1-8)
5. Establishment of a world church (Revelation 17:1-15)
6. Russia springs a surprise attack on Israel four years before the second coming of Christ (Ezekiel 38-39)
7. Peace treaty with Israel broken after 3 1/2 years: beginning of one-world government, one-world economic system, one-world atheistic religion, final 3 1/2 years before second coming of Christ (Daniel 7:23; Revelation 13:5-8,15-17; 17:16-17)
8. Many Christians and Jews martyred who refused to worship world dictator (Revelation 7:9-17; 13:15)
9. Catastrophic divine judgments represented by seals, trumpets, and bowls poured out on the earth (Revelation 6-18)
10. World war breaks out focusing on the Middle East: Battle of Armageddon (Daniel 11:40-45; Revelation 9:13-21; 16:12-16)
11. Babylon destroyed (Revelation 18)
12. Second coming of Christ (Matthew 24:27-31; Revelation 19:11-21)
13. Judgment of wicked Jews and Gentiles (Ezekiel 20:33–38; Matthew 25:31-46; Jude 14-15; Revelation 19:15-21; 20:1-4)
14. Satan bound for 1,000 years (Revelation 20:1-3)
15. Resurrection of Tribulation saints and Old Testament saints (Daniel 12:2; Revelation 20:4)
16. Millennial kingdom begins (Revelation 20:5-6)
17. Final rebellion at the end of the Millennium (Revelation 20:7-10)
18. Resurrection and final judgment of the wicked: Great White Throne judgment (Revelation 20:11-15)
19. Eternity begins: new heaven, new earth, New Jerusalem (Revelation 21:1-2)

* Taken from John F. Walvoord, *The Prophecy Knowledge Handbook*, Wheaton, IL: Victor

prior to the Great Tribulation judgments (Revelation 3:10).

- The *rise of the Antichrist* and the *False Prophet* to control the New World Order of the end times (Revelation 13:1-4; 11-8).
- The *tribulation period* on the earth with widespread ecological destruction, war, and famine (Matthew 24:21-22).
- The *triumphal return of Christ* with His church to overthrow the Antichrist and bind Satan for 1,000 years (Revelation 19:11-16; 20:1-2).
- The *millennial kingdom* of Christ on earth for 1,000 years of peace and prosperity (Revelation 5:10; 20:4-6).

Beyond these key events, we can only speculate about what will happen. The Bible seems to predict an age of unparalleled selfism in the last days (2 Timothy 3:1-6). It seems to indicate an age of skepticism and unbelief; a time when people will scoff at the idea of Christ's return (2 Peter 3:3-4). It also appears that this age will be marked by global wealth and prosperity (Revelation 18:11-19).

THE NEXT GENERATION

The next generation could well be the last one on planet earth. Social issues like poverty, prejudice, and racial hatred continue to plague our world. The riots in our nation's cities only serve to underscore the depth of racial tension in our own country. In the meantime, racial, ethnic, and religious conflict threaten to tear apart Eastern Europe and the Commonwealth of Independent States that make up the former Soviet Union. All indications are that the years ahead will be marked by the widespread production of nuclear bombs by Third World nations, some of which are led by trigger-happy, egotistical military dictators. And all of this is taking place in the midst of continued deterioration of the earth's atmosphere and environment.

We can only *speculate* about what will happen in the years ahead. My guess is that we will see these trends:

1. *America* will be in serious danger of becoming a second-rate nation overburdened with economic struggles.

2. The success of the *New Europe* will put pressure on the United States to join forces economically and, eventually, politically with the New World Order.

3. The *United Nations* will be used as the means to bring about a world government that supersedes individual national interests. America will submit her national interests as well to the World State.

4. *Computerized transfers* will eliminate the need for cash. The long-awaited cashless society will become a reality in the future.

5. *World economic control* will be centralized on the European continent. In time, all financial transactions will be controlled at a central agency.

6. Despite the initial success of global economic unity, a *worldwide economic disaster* will occur, increasing the need for further global economic controls, including a personalized insignia.

7. The threat of a *global nuclear holocaust* will push the world to the brink of disaster and leave people crying for peace. This crisis will probably be centered in the Middle East.

8. *A prominent world leader* will emerge who is able to bring peace to the planet. In time, he will sign a major peace treaty with Israel.

9. However, he will *break that treaty* and turn against Israel, attempting to drive the Jewish people out of their land. Worldwide chaos will develop, and the world leader will find himself embroiled in a great military conflict.

10. The world will again be pushed to the *brink of disaster* as the armies of the nations attack one another at Armageddon.

WHAT CAN WE DO NOW?

Personal preparation for the return of Christ is a decision each individual must make for himself. I also believe there are collective decisions we can make as a people and a nation. We must readjust several of our priorities immediately. Today's evangelical Christian church is too preoccupied with itself. Today's Christians are sidetracked on self-indulgence. Self-help books dominate the Christian bookstores. God's people are into themselves—their identity, success, and money. We need to realize there is no lasting future for a temporal and material world.

It is time for Christians to see the big picture again. The world is in serious trouble, and we alone can help people see their spiritual needs. We must take seriously our Lord's command to evangelize all the nations before the end comes (Matthew 28:19-20).

What are Christians to do? First, we must *evangelize the world* as never before. We must train young people to reach the world in their lifetime. We must train thousands of young men and women to carry the gospel message around the globe through whatever professions they choose. We need doctors, lawyers, missionaries, engineers, teachers, coaches, nurses, counselors, athletes, musicians, businessmen, politicians, and preachers who will use their respective platforms to evangelize the world.

There are many legitimate avenues of service for believers, but none is more crucial than evangelism. We must reach the next generation for Christ. This present age may well be our last opportunity to do so before it is too late.

Second, we must *infiltrate every walk of life* with faithful and dynamic Christians. If we want to make an impact on society, we cannot do so by avoiding unbelievers. Just as the early Christians "conquered" the Roman Empire from within, we must do the same. Christians ought to strive to be the very best they can within their fields of endeavor. There is no reason why we cannot produce the best writers, journalists, doctors, lawyers, technicians, teachers, and leaders in American society.

Third, we must *revitalize the ministry of the local church.* We can reach today's generation only by revitalized ministries that are aimed at today's people. Please note that I am not saying we need to compromise our *message.* Rather, we must adjust our *methods* to meet the needs of today's young couples, singles, teenagers, and adults. This is never an easy adjustment for older believers, but we must continue to keep our music, worship, preaching, and teaching relevant to the entire spectrum of people whom we are trying to evangelize and disciple.

Fourth, we must remain *vigilant on the moral issues of our times.* After a decade and a half of raising the moral conscience of our nation, it would be easy to let down. Some Christians are tired of hearing about abortion, drugs, pornography, and homosexuality, but these issues simply will not go away. We cannot let down now. As Will Scarlett asked Robin Hood, "Are you going to finish what you started?" Likewise we must ask ourselves, "Are we willing to stand by the truth until we have finally won the battle?"

Fifth, we must continue to *remain active in the political process.* Since 1980, Christians have made a difference in nearly every major election in this country. We are a force with which to be reckoned. Of course, electing the right presidents, senators, and congressmen alone won't solve our national problems. But it is a step in the right direction. It sure beats electing the wrong kind of people to office. It is better for Christians to be able to work *with* the political system than *against* it.

LIVING ON THE EDGE

In our Lord's final instructions to the church, He said we were to serve as *witnesses* for Him (Acts 1:8), and *evangelize* the whole world (Matthew 28:19-20). His plan could not be more clear. He gave no exceptions. He allowed no detours. He told us exactly what to do until He returned.

Yet today's churches have found it difficult to stay on course with our Lord's instructions. We get so busy doing other tasks that we often overlook the main task to which we are called. Yes, we are to baptize, teach, instruct, and train those who are converted. But we are to conduct those ministries as a follow up to evangelism, not in place of evangelism.

In addition to winning people to Christ, we must live our Christianity with integrity and authenticity. Today's generation is fervently questioning religion. People honestly want to know who and what is for real.

Living on the edge for Christ reminds us that our real destiny is in heaven. When we become too comfortable here on earth, we lose our sense of urgency over Christ's return. We are to exhaust ourselves in His service, expend our resources, and give that last full measure of devotion so that we can lie down on the battlefield of life knowing we have done our best by the grace of God.

We could well be entering the ninth inning of the game of life. This is not the time to put away the bats, balls, and gloves. This is not the time to head for the showers. The game isn't over yet! You and I may still be called upon to step to the plate and deliver a key hit one more time before the heavenly Father calls the game.

Chapter 13

⟨✳⟩

IT ISN'T OVER
TILL IT'S OVER

One of the great baseball minds of all time, Yogi Berra, used to say, "It ain't over till it's over!" He was referring to the unpredictable endings in athletic events. Just when the ball game appears to be down to the last easy, predictable out, anything and everything can start happening.

The same is true about trying to relate current events to Bible prophecy. Just when you think you have it all figured out, something unexpected happens. Nobody was prepared for the sudden and spontaneous collapse of communism all over Eastern Europe. I cannot think of one prophecy writer who anticipated such a chain of events happening so quickly. Nobody, other than the Israelis, took Saddam Hussein as a serious threat in the Middle East. Prophecy speculators warned us about Iran, Egypt, and Libya, but hardly anyone talked about Iraq, and some people had never even heard of Kuwait.

As incomprehensible as it seems, some of the world's greatest crises have been precipitated in some of the most obscure places: the assassination of the Austrian archduke in Sarajevo,

Yugoslavia, was the spark that ignited World War I; the German invasion of Czechoslovakia began the chain of events that led to World War II; the remote jungles of Vietnam took away American pride and confidence for a long time to come; and the invasion of the tiny kingdom of Kuwait brought about the greatest mobilization of military forces since World War II.

All of that makes us wonder how the world will end someday. Perhaps in some obscure outpost of humanity, the spark will be lit that leads to Armageddon. That spark may even seem an insignificant event at first, but then, like the beginnings of a great conflagration, the flames of hatred will quickly spread out of control and the world will find itself on the verge of extinction.

WHERE WILL IT ALL END?

The Bible warns us that humanity is marching toward inevitable destruction. The end might not come now or even in our lifetimes, but one day it *will* come. Scripture tells us that the great crisis will begin somewhere in the Middle East and eventually spread to the whole world.

The prophet Isaiah warned of a day when God would judge the whole earth (Isaiah 24).[1] He foresaw a time when God would "lay waste the earth and devastate it. . . . The earth will be completely laid waste and totally plundered. . . . The earth dries up and withers, the world languishes. . . . earth's inhabitants are burned up, and very few are left" (Isaiah 24:1-6).

There can be little doubt that Isaiah is talking about the Great Tribulation, which will culminate in the Battle of Armageddon.[2] He sees a world in which God's wrath is being poured on "all nations" (Isaiah 34:2) and where the "mountains shall be melted" (Isaiah 34:3 KJV) and the "stars of heaven will be dissolved and the sky rolled up like a scroll" (Isaiah 34:4).

In both Isaiah 24 and 34, the prophet sees ahead to the time of God's judgment on the whole world. While Scripture records specific judgments on Israel during the "time of Jacob's trouble" and on the kingdom of the Antichrist, symbolically called

Babylon, it also tells us that an even greater judgment will come upon the world at large. No person or place shall escape God's retribution at the end time. This apocalyptic holocaust will be worldwide and no one will be able to hide from what God has waiting for them.

How Will It All End?

The question of *how* this will all come about divides Christians who have differing eschatological views. *Pre-Tribulationists* believe that Christ will rapture the church to heaven prior to the Great Tribulation and then return with His bride at the end of the Tribulation to set up His kingdom on earth. *Mid-* and *post-Tribulationists* believe the church will suffer to some extent during the tribulation period and be caught up at a midpoint or at the very end of the Great Tribulation.

Amillennialists believe that things will get worse at the end of the church age. While most people view the entire church age as a time of tribulation for believers, some feel that the persecution of the Christians will get worse in the last days. Amillennialists say that at the very end, the Battle of Armageddon will commence and Christ will return to judge the world and usher in eternity.

Postmillennialists believe that the church is the kingdom of God on earth and that it is our responsibility to bring in the kingdom by the preaching of the gospel and the enactment of Christian laws, values, and principles in society until the whole world is converted to Christ.

Obviously there are great differences in each of those views and yet each one contains an element of truth that all Christians need to remember. From the *pre-Tribulationalist* we are reminded to be ready for the coming of Christ at any moment. From the *mid-* and *post-Tribulationists* we are reminded that frequently Christians are called to suffer for Christ. Certainly, believers in the Third World could teach us much about what it means to suffer for Christ.

The *amillennialist* reminds us that we must be ready to face the judgment of God. While it is exciting to think about our Lord's coming, we must also realize that His judgment is coming as well. While we premillennialists look forward to Christ's earthly kingdom, we must also remember that even that will come to an end and be merged into the eternal kingdom of God. The apostle Paul says there is coming a time when Christ "hands over the kingdom to God the Father" (1 Corinthians 15:24).

From the *postmillennialist* we are reminded of our Christian responsibilities to the world in which we live. Since we do not know the exact time of Christ's return, we dare not sit back and do nothing but wait for the rapture. Christ has given us specific orders about our responsibilities to one another and to the world at large. We are called to be the light of the world and the salt of the earth until our Lord returns (Matthew 5:13-16).

When Will It All End?

The Bible clearly states that no one but God knows the exact time of the end of the age (Matthew 24:36). Therefore, even the most sincerely calculated guesses are destined to fail. The clues given in Scripture are these:

1. *When the gospel has been preached to the whole world,* "then the end will come" (Matthew 24:14). This indicates our mandate to continue evangelizing until Jesus comes again (Matthew 28:19-20).
2. *When the bride of Christ (the church) is complete* and the last convert has been added, Christ will come for His church. Jesus said, "I go and prepare a place for you, I will come back and take you to be with me that you also may be where I am" (John 14:3).
3. *When the church is raptured to heaven,* the church age will close. Paul said, "We who are still alive and are left will be caught up together with them in the clouds to meet the Lord in the air. And so we will be with the Lord forever" (1 Thessalonians 4:17).

4. *When the "times of the Gentiles" have been completed,* God will once again deal with Israel as His people on earth. Jesus said to His disciples, "Jerusalem will be trampled on by the Gentiles until the times of the Gentiles are fulfilled" (Luke 21:24; cf. Zechariah 14:1-9).

5. *When the marriage of Christ and the church is finalized,* believers will be in a perfect and fixed moral state for all eternity. In the present era, the church is engaged to Christ (2 Corinthians 11:2) in a relationship that is so binding it is described as marriage (Ephesians 5:21-33). After the rapture, the bride will be made ready for the marriage supper in heaven (Revelation 19:1-8).

WHAT SHOULD WE BE DOING?

Since we can never be sure when God's purposes for His church will be finalized, we must remain obedient to our Lord's commands regarding His church. This was made clear to the disciples at the time of Christ's ascension to heaven. They had asked if He was going to restore the kingdom to Israel at that time, and Jesus told them, "It is not for you to know the times or dates the Father has set by His own authority" (Acts 1:7). Two facts are clear in this statement: 1) The date has been set; 2) we aren't supposed to know it because we have a responsibility to fulfill in the meantime.

In the very next verse, Jesus gave the Great Commission, telling the disciples they would be empowered by the Holy Spirit to be His witnesses in Jerusalem, Judea, Samaria, and "to the ends of the earth" (Acts 1:8). Then, to their amazement, He ascended into heaven, leaving them gazing intently into the sky. Two men in white (probably angels) appeared and asked, "Why do you stand here looking into the sky? This same Jesus, who has been taken from you into heaven, will come back in the same way you have seen him go into heaven" (Acts 1:11).

All too often, today's Christians are just like those early disciples. We spend more time gazing into the sky and speculating about Christ's return than we do serving Him. The angels' point was to remind the disciples that His return is certain. Thus we shouldn't waste time and energy worrying about when or whether Christ will return. Believe that He is coming again on schedule and be about His business in the meantime.

Jesus left several instructions about what we ought to be doing while we await His coming:

1. *Witness for Him everywhere you go.* Our Lord told His disciples to be His witnesses everywhere that they go, even to the farthest ends of the earth (Acts 1:8).

2. *"Go into all the world and preach the good news"* (Mark 16:15). This command emphasizes the evangelistic and missionary nature of the church's ministry during the present era. We are to take the gospel to the whole world.

3. *"Repentance and forgiveness of sins will be preached . . . to all nations"* our Lord declared in Luke 24:47. Calling men and women to repent and believe the gospel is the twofold nature of the evangelistic enterprise.

4. *"Make disciples of all nations, baptizing them,"* Jesus said in Matthew 28:19. Making converts and discipling them in their walk with God is a major emphasis of the church's mission.

5. *Build the church, not fearing the gates of hell.* Jesus told His disciples that He would build His church with such power that "the gates of hell shall not prevail against it" (Matthew 16:18 KJV). We usually act as though hell were attacking the church and we were trying to survive. But remember, you don't attack with gates. You defend with gates. Jesus pictured the church on the offensive and hell on the defensive.

6. *"Occupy till I come"* (Luke 19:13 KJV), Jesus said in the parable of the talents. In this parable, the servants were to "put this money to work" until their master returned. We are to stay busy about the Master's business until He returns.

7. *Remain faithful until He returns.* Our Lord concluded His prophetic message in the Olivet Discourse by reminding His disciples to continue in faithful and wise service even though He might be gone a long time (Matthew 24:45-51; 25:14-21).

THE END HAS ALREADY BEGUN

Almost 2,000 years ago, the apostle Peter said, "The end of all things is near. Therefore be clear minded and self-controlled so that you can pray" (1 Peter 4:7). Way back in the New Testament era Peter and the other apostles sensed that they had moved dramatically closer to the consummation of God's plan for this world. The Old Testament age had come to an end, and they were now part of a new era.

Peter's reference to the end is expressed by a perfect tense verb in the original Greek text. This means the action involved is a present reality with future consequences. It could just as appropriately be translated, "The end of all things has already begun." For Peter, the end of the age was already a present reality.

The first coming of Christ initiated the end of the age (*see* Acts 2:14-20 and Hebrews 1:2), and His second coming will terminate the end of the age (Matthew 24:30). Therefore, the entire church age is a last days in a general sense. And the very end of those days is a specific last days, or a last of the last days.

Scripture also speaks of the end as a future event. The apostle Paul predicted, "There will be terrible times in the last days" (2 Timothy 3:1). The opening verse of the Apocalypse refers to "things which must shortly come to pass" (Revelation 1:1 KJV) and goes on to warn us that "the time is near" (Revelation 1:3). Scripture also presents Christ's coming as an imminent reality. "Behold, I am coming soon!" Christ promised (Revelation 22:7). He will come suddenly, and He could come at any moment.

The ominous events of the recent Persian Gulf War remind us all of how quickly an international crisis of great magnitude can erupt in the Middle East. While other conflicts around the world may come and go, the Bible focuses on the Middle East as the place where the ultimate conflict will take place.

WHAT TIME IS IT?

That leaves us asking this question: What time is it now? Peter referred to the *present,* saying, "[Christ] was revealed in these last times" (1 Peter 1:20). At the same time, Peter referred to the coming of Christ as a future event "ready to be revealed in the last time" (1 Peter 1:5). It is clear that he viewed the last times as both a present reality and a future event.

The Bible affirms three basic facts about the coming of Christ and the end of the age.

First, *we are living in the last days.* Every generation of Christians has lived with the hope of the imminent return of Christ. We believe that He could return at any moment. There is no prophetic event that remains to be fulfilled before the way can be opened for Him to return. In fact, certain events, like the return of Israel to her land, indicate that we are closer to the end than ever before.

Second, *God's timetable is not our timetable.* Peter himself told us that "in the last days scoffers will come," questioning the promise of His second coming (2 Peter 3:3-4). They will reject the idea of God's intervention in His creation and suggest that all things are moving forward at their own pace without God. These skeptics will also fail to anticipate God's coming judgment upon the world (2 Peter 3:7). In this context Peter reminds us, "With the Lord a day is like a thousand years, and a thousand years are like a day" (2 Peter 3:8). God's perspective is not limited to human time. According to God's timetable, Jesus has been back in heaven for less than two days! Don't mistake the patience of God for a change in His plans. He is waiting, giving His people time to repent. The Bible warns, "He who is coming will come and will not delay" (Hebrews 10:37).

Third, *Christ's coming is closer than it has ever been.* The Bible emphatically promises that Christ is coming again (Luke 12:40;

Philippians 3:20; Titus 2:13; Hebrews 9:28). Scripture urges us to be watching, waiting, and ready for our Lord to return. Every day that passes brings us one day closer. Whether He returns next week or 1,000 years from now, we are to be living as though He were coming today.

How Should We Live?

The hope of the second coming is the strongest encouragement for us to live right until Jesus comes. The apostle John said, "Continue in him, so that when he appears we may be confident and unashamed before him at his coming. . . . we know that when he appears, we shall be like him for we shall see him as he is. Everyone who has this hope in him purifies himself, just as he is pure" (1 John 2:28; 3:2-3).

The ultimate incentive to right living is the fact that we will face our Lord when He comes again. No matter what our failures and mistakes in the past, each of us needs to be ready when He comes. How, then, should we live?

First, *you need to know Jesus Christ personally*. The whole purpose of our Lord's first coming was to die as the atoning sacrifice for our sins. He came to pay the price for our sins so that we might be forgiven and released from the penalty of eternal death. He is called the Redeemer because He has redeemed us from God's judgment against our sin. Peter said, "You were redeemed . . . with the precious blood of Christ. . . . He was chosen before the creation of the world, but was revealed in these last times for your sake. Through him you believe in God, who raised him from the dead and glorified him, and so your faith and hope are in God" (1 Peter 1:18-21).

Second, *you need to commit your life to Him by faith*. We cannot earn salvation by our own good works, nor is it something we deserve. It must be received as a free gift from God. The Bible says, "Christ died for sins once for all, the righteous for the unrighteous, to bring you to God" (1 Peter 3:18). The gospel—good news—is the message that Christ died for our

NAMES OF CHRIST IN REVELATION

᠓᠕᠍᠍᠑   ᠓᠕᠑   ᠓᠕᠑

The book of Revelation was designed to close the New Testament revelation and to be the final inspired statement from God until the return of Christ Himself. The theme of the book is the revelation of the person and the prophetic program of Jesus Christ.

A number of purposes can be detected in the book. First, it was written to encourage believers to endure persecution and to persevere through suffering, knowing that the victory of Christ over the world and the devil is certain. Second, the book was written to show how all of prophecy focuses on Jesus Christ—His person and His program for the world.

This book lists more titles for the Savior than does any other book in the Bible. Here are but a few:

1. Jesus Christ (1:1)
2. Faithful Witness (1:5)
3. First Begotten of the dead (1:5)
4. Prince of kings of the earth (1:5)
5. Alpha and Omega (1:8)
6. First and the last (1:7)
7. Son of man (1:13)
8. Son of God (2:18)
9. Keeper of David's keys (3:7)
10. Keeper of the keys of hell and death (1:18)
11. Lion of the tribe of Judah (5:5)
12. Root of David (5:5)
13. Slain Lamb (5:6)
14. Angry Lamb (6:16-17)
15. Tender Lamb (7:17)
16. Our Lord (11:8)
17. The man Child (12:5)
18. King of saints (15:3)
19. Faithful and True (19:11)
20. Word of God (19:13)
21. King of kings (19:16)
22. Lord of lords (19:16)
23. Beginning and the End (22:13)
24. Bright and Morning Star (22:16)

* Taken from *Willmington's Guide to the Bible*, Wheaton, IL: Tyndale House, 1986, pp. 275-276. Used with permission.

sins, was buried, and rose again (1 Corinthians 15:3-4). The invitation of the gospel calls us to personal faith in those facts. The Bible says, "To all who received him, to those who believed in his name, he gave the right to become children of God" (John 1:12).

Third, *you need to surrender to His lordship.* Jesus Christ said that He came into the world to save sinners and call them to be His disciples. He further commissioned those disciples to go into the whole world and make more disciples, calling them to accountability to the lordship of Christ (Matthew 28:19-20). We are encouraged to be "clear minded and self-controlled" (1 Peter 4:7) so that we may serve the Lord Jesus faithfully.

HOW CAN WE BE READY?

There are many things that demand our attention in life. There are many voices calling to us and many images that flash across the screens of our minds. But no matter what our focus in life, one thing is certain: All of us will face death at some point. We cannot avoid it. All of us are vulnerable.

Death is the great equalizer. It makes no difference how rich or poor, famous or infamous, respected or rejected you may have been in this life. When you face death you are facing an impartial judge. The Bible reminds us that "all have sinned" (Romans 3:23) and the "wages of sin is death" (Romans 6:23). When death comes knocking at your door, all that really matters is that you are ready to face it.

"How can I be ready?" Tom asked me recently. "I know that I am running out of time." He had been fighting conviction and resisting God for quite a while.

"You must respond by faith to God's promise to save you," I replied. "Christ died for your sins and rose from the dead to give you eternal life. Trusting Him for your salvation means believing that when He died, He died for you and that when He rose, He rose for you. The basic invitation of Scripture says, 'Everyone who calls on the name of the Lord will be saved' " (Romans 10:13).

"Have you ever asked Him to save you and believed that He would?" I asked.

"No, not really," Tom replied, lowering his head.

"Would you like to ask Him to forgive your sins, save your soul, and take you to heaven?" I asked further.

"Yes, I would!" he said emphatically.

As we bowed our heads and prayed, he called upon the Lord Jesus Christ by faith to save him and believed He did.

When we finished praying together, Tom looked at me and said, "Now I'm ready because I believe He will keep His promise to me."

You can have that same kind of assurance in your life. You may have been drawn to an interest in prophecies of the end times so that you could think through the question of your own future destiny. Perhaps you've heard people talk about Armageddon, the coming of Christ, and the end of the age, and you've realized that you are not ready to meet Him when He comes. Perhaps you have recognized that the end could come at any moment and you are not prepared to step into eternity.

There is no better time to settle the question of your own eternal destiny than right now. John the Baptist called Jesus "the Lamb of God, who takes away the sin of the world" (John 1:29). Won't you let Him take away your sin? Bow your heart, soul, mind, and head before Him and ask Him to save you right now.

When Billy Graham was asked on a popular television show to summarize what his life and ministry were all about, he simply quoted John 3:16: "For God so loved the world that he gave his one and only Son, that whoever believes in him shall not perish but have eternal life."

The clock of human history is ticking away. It neither speeds up nor slows down. It just keeps on ticking continually and relentlessly, moving us closer and closer to the end of the age. How close we are to the end will only be revealed by time itself. Don't gamble with your eternal destiny. Time may very well be running out. Make sure you are ready when Jesus comes.

APPENDIX

25 Major Prophecies
of the End Times

The prophecies in this appendix are listed in 25 categories and taken directly from Scripture. These are for personal study and easy cross-reference. The Bible is the only source of the "sure word of prophecy" (2 Peter 2:19 KJV). And God's Word is the only true prophecy of future events. More important than human opinion is what God says about the future. Search these scriptures for yourself and pray that God will open your mind to understand what the Spirit has revealed about the end times.

1. *Spread of the Gospel Message and Growth of the Church*

I will build my church, and the gates of Hades will not overcome it (Matthew 24:14).

This gospel of the kingdom will be preached in the whole world as a testimony to all nations, and then the end will come (Matthew 16:18).

The kingdom of heaven is like a mustard seed, which a man took and planted in his field. Though it is the smallest of all your seeds, yet when it grows, it is the largest of garden plants and becomes a tree (Matthew 13:31-32).

2. *Increase of Wickedness and the Spread of Evil*

Because of the increase of wickedness, the love of most will grow cold (Matthew 24:12.)

But mark this: There will be terrible times in the last days. People will be lovers of themselves, lovers of money, boastful, proud, abusive, disobedient to their parents, ungrateful, unholy, without love, unforgiving, slanderous, without self-control, brutal, not lovers of the good, treacherous, rash, conceited, lovers of pleasure rather than lovers of God—having a form of godliness but denying its power (2 Timothy 3:1-5).

First of all, you must understand that in the last days scoffers will come, scoffing and following their own evil desires. They will say, "Where is this 'coming' he promised? (2 Peter 3:3-4).

Remember what the apostles of our Lord Jesus Christ foretold. They said to you, "In the last times there will be scoffers who will follow their own ungodly desires" (Jude 17-18).

3. *Rise of False Prophets and Apostate Religion*

The Spirit clearly says that in later times some will abandon the faith and follow deceiving spirits and things taught by demons (1 Timothy 4:1).

Jesus answered: "Watch out that no one deceives you. For many will come in my name, claiming, 'I am the Christ,' and will deceive many. . . . For false Christs and false prophets will appear and perform great signs and miracles to deceive even the elect—if that were possible" (Matthew 24:4,24).

There were also false prophets among the people, just as there will be false teachers among you. They will secretly introduce destructive heresies. . . . In their greed these teachers will exploit you with stories they have made up (2 Peter 2:1-3).

For such men are false apostles, deceitful workmen, masquerading as apostles of Christ. And no wonder, for Satan himself masquerades as an angel of light (2 Corinthians 11:13-14).

4. *Continuation of "the Times of the Gentiles"*

Jerusalem will be trampled on by the Gentiles until the times of the Gentiles are fulfilled (Luke 21:24).

I do not want you to be ignorant of this mystery, brothers . . . Israel has experienced a hardening in part until the full number of the Gentiles has come in (Romans 11:25).

I ask then: Did God reject his people? By no means! . . . at the present time there is a remnant chosen by grace (Romans 11:1,5).

How long will it be before these astonishing things are fulfilled. . . . It will be for a time, times and half a time. When the power of the holy people has been finally broken, all these things will be completed (Daniel 12:6-7).

5. *Return of Israel to the Land*

I will bring you from the nations and gather you from the countries where you have been scattered (Ezekiel 20:34).

Therefore prophesy and say to them: "This is what the Sovereign LORD says: O my people, I am going to open your graves and bring you up from them; I will bring you back to the land of Israel. . . . and I will settle you in your own land" (Ezekiel 37:12,14).

This is what the Sovereign LORD says: I will take the Israelites out of the nations where they have gone. I will gather them from all around and bring them back into their own land (Ezekiel 37:21).

I will bring your children from the east and gather you from the west. I will say to the north, "Give them up!" and to the south, "Do not hold them back." Bring my sons from afar and my daughters from the ends of the earth (Isaiah 43:5-6).

I will bring back my exiled people Israel; they will rebuild the ruined cities and live in them (Amos 9:14).

6. *Conflict in the Middle East*

When you see Jerusalem being surrounded by armies, you will know that its desolation is near. . . . For this is the time of punishment in fulfillment of all that has been written (Luke 21:20,22).

The word of the LORD came to me: "Son of man, set your face against Gog, of the land of Magog, the chief prince of Meshech and Tubal. . . . Persia, Cush, and Put will be with them . . . also Gomer with all its troops, and Beth Togarmah from the far north with all its troops—the many nations with you" (Ezekiel 38:1-2,5-6).

I will gather all nations and bring them down to the Valley of Jehoshaphat. . . . Proclaim this among the nations: Prepare for war! . . . Multitudes, multitudes in the valley of decision! For the day of the LORD is near in the valley of decision (Joel 3:2,9,14).

You will hear of wars and rumors of wars, but see to it that you are not alarmed. Such things must happen, but the end is still to come. Nation will rise against nation, and kingdom against kingdom (Matthew 24:6-7).

7. *The Rapture of the Church*

If I go and prepare a place for you, I will come back and take you to be with me that you also may be where I am (John 14:3).

I will also keep you from the hour of trial that is going to come upon the whole world (Revelation 3:10).

Concerning the coming of our Lord Jesus Christ and our being gathered to him, we ask you, brothers, not to become easily unsettled or alarmed (2 Thessalonians 2:1-2).

The dead in Christ will rise first. After that, we who are still alive and are left will be caught up together with them in the clouds to meet the Lord in the air (1 Thessalonians 4:16-17).

Listen, I tell you a mystery: We will not all sleep, but we will all be changed—in a flash, in the twinkling of an eye, at the last trumpet. For the trumpet will sound, the dead will be raised imperishable, and we will be changed (1 Corinthians 15:51-52).

They came to life and reigned with Christ a thousand years. . . . This is the first resurrection (Revelation 20:4-5).

8. *Marriage of Christ and the Church in Heaven*

Let us rejoice and be glad and give him glory! For the wedding of the Lamb has come and his bride has made herself ready (Revelation 19:7).

I am jealous for you with a godly jealousy. I promised you to one husband, to Christ, so that I might present you as a pure virgin to him (2 Corinthians 11:2).

Husbands, love your wives, just as Christ loved the church and gave himself up for her to make her holy . . . and to present her to himself as a radiant church, without stain or wrinkle or any other blemish, but holy and blameless (Ephesians 5:25-27).

At midnight the cry rang out: "Here's the bridegroom! Come out to meet him!" (Matthew 25:6).

9. *Rise of the Antichrist and the False Prophet*

Don't let anyone deceive you in any way, for that day will not come until the rebellion occurs and the man of lawlessness is revealed, the man doomed to destruction. He will oppose and will exalt himself over everything that is called God or is worshiped, so that he sets himself up in God's temple, proclaiming himself to be God. . . . And then the lawless one will be revealed, whom the Lord Jesus will overthrow with the breath of his mouth and destroy by the splendor of his coming (2 Thessalonians 2:3-4,8).

Who is the liar? It is the man who denies that Jesus is

the Christ. Such a man is the antichrist—he denies the Father and the Son (1 John 2:22).

I saw a beast coming out of the sea. He had ten horns and seven heads. . . . resembled a leopard . . . a bear . . . a lion. The dragon gave the beast his power and his throne and great authority. . . . The whole world was astonished and followed the beast . . . . and they also worshiped the beast and asked, "Who is like the beast? Who can make war against him?"(Revelation 13:1-4).

I saw another beast, coming out of the earth. He had two horns like a lamb, but he spoke like a dragon. He . . . made the earth and its inhabitants worship the first beast . . . . he deceived the inhabitants of the earth. He ordered them to set up an image in honor of the beast. . . . He also forced everyone, small and great, rich and poor, free and slave, to receive a mark on his right hand or on his forehead, so that no one could buy or sell unless he had the mark, which is the name of the beast or the number of his name. . . . 666 (Revelation 13:11-18).

10. *Development of a Global Economy*

He also forced everyone, small and great, rich and poor, free and slave, to receive a mark on his right hand or on his forehead, so that no one could buy or sell unless he had the mark, which is the name of the beast or the number of his name (Revelation 13:16-17).

The merchants of the earth grew rich from [Babylon's] excessive luxuries. . . . The merchants of the earth will weep and mourn over her because no one buys their cargoes any more—cargoes of gold, silver, precious stones and pearls; fine linen, purple, silk and scarlet cloth; every sort of citron wood, and articles of every kind made of ivory, costly wood, bronze, iron and marble. . . . Your merchants were the world's great men. By your magic spell all the nations were led astray (Revelation 18:3, 11-12, 23).

11. *Formation of a World Government*

It will be different from all the other kingdoms and will devour the whole earth, trampling it down and crushing it (Daniel 7:23).

All inhabitants of the earth will worship the beast—all whose names have not been written in the book of life belonging to the Lamb that was slain from the creation of the world (Revelation 13:8).

He exercised all the authority of the first beast on his behalf, and made the earth and its inhabitants worship the first beast, whose fatal wound had been healed (Revelation 13:12).

Come I will show you . . . the great prostitute, who sits on many waters. . . . The waters you saw, where the prostitute sits, are peoples, multitudes, nations and languages . . . . The woman you saw is the great city that rules over the kings of the earth (Revelation 17:1,15,18).

12. *Sense of False Peace and Security*

"Peace, peace," they say, when there is no peace (Jeremiah 6:14).

You know very well that the day of the Lord will come like a thief in the night. While people are saying, "Peace and safety," destruction will come on them suddenly, as labor pains on a pregnant woman, and they will not escape (1 Thessalonians 5:2-3).

13. *Development of Weapons of Mass Destruction*

Another horse came out, a fiery red one. Its rider was given power to take peace from the earth and to make men slay each other. To him was given a large sword (Revelation 6:4).

The sun turned black like sackcloth made of goat hair, the whole moon turned blood red, and the stars in the sky fell to earth. . . . The sky receded like a scroll, rolling up, and every mountain and island was removed from its place (Revelation 6:12-14).

The day of the Lord will come like a thief. The heavens will disappear with a roar; the elements will be destroyed by fire, and the earth and everything in it will be laid bare (2 Peter 3:10).

The first angel sounded his trumpet, and there came hail and fire mixed with blood, and it was hurled down upon the earth. A third of the earth was burned up, a third of the trees were burned up, and all the green grass was burned up (Revelation 8:7).

The number of the mounted troops was two hundred million. . . . out of their mouths came fire, smoke and sulfur. A third of mankind was killed by the three plagues of fire, smoke and sulfur that came out of their mouths (Revelation 9:16-18).

14. *Environmental Disasters*

Something like a huge mountain all ablaze, was thrown into the sea. . . . a third of all the living creatures in the sea died . . . a great star, blazing like a torch, fell from the sky . . . . a third of the waters turned bitter, and many people died. . . . the sun was struck . . . the moon . . . the stars. . . . A third of the day was without light, and also a third of the night (Revelation 8:8-12).

Ugly and painful sores broke out on the people . . . . the sea . . . turned into blood . . . and every living thing in the sea died. . . . the rivers and springs of water . . . became blood . . . . the sun was given power to scorch people with fire. . . . and they cursed the name of God (Revelation 16:2-8).

15. *Judgments of the Tribulation Period*

There will be a time of distress such as has not happened from the beginning of nations until then (Daniel 12:1).

The great day of the LORD is near—near and coming quickly. . . . That day will be a day of wrath, a day of distress and anguish, a day of trouble and ruin, a day of darkness and gloom, a day of clouds and blackness. . . . In the fire of his jealousy the whole world will be consumed, for he will make a sudden end of all who live in the earth (Zephaniah 1:14-15,18).

There will be great distress, unequaled from the beginning of the world until now—and never to be equaled again. If those days had not been cut short, no one would survive, but for the sake of the elect those days will be shortened (Matthew 24:22).

How awful that day will be! None will be like it. It will be a time of trouble for Jacob, but he will be saved out of it (Jeremiah 30:7).

See, the LORD is going to lay waste the earth and devastate it; he will ruin its face and scatter its inhabitants. . . . The earth is broken up, the earth is split asunder, the earth is thoroughly shaken. The earth reels like a drunkard, it sways like a hut in the wind (Isaiah 24:1,19-20).

You know very well that the day of the Lord will come like a thief in the night. While people are saying, "Peace and safety," destruction will come on them suddenly, as labor pains on a pregnant woman, and they will not escape (1 Thessalonians 5:1-3).

They called to the mountains and the rocks, "Fall on us and hide us from the face of him who sits on the throne and from the wrath of the Lamb! For the great day of their wrath has come, and who can stand?"(Revelation 6:16-17).

16. *Conversion of Israel*

I will make known my holy name among my people Israel. . . . It is coming! It will surely take place, declares the Sovereign LORD. This is the day I have spoken of (Ezekiel 39:7-8).

I will pour out on the house of David and the inhabitants of Jerusalem a spirit of grace and supplication. They will look on me, the one they have pierced, and they will mourn for him as one mourns for an only child, and grieve bitterly for him as one grieves for a firstborn son (Zechariah 12:10).

On that day a fountain will be opened to the house of David and the inhabitants of Jerusalem, to cleanse them from sin and impurity. . . . If someone asks him, "What are these wounds on your body?" he will answer, "The wounds I was given at the house of my friends" (Zechariah 13:1,6).

Israel has experienced a hardening in part until the full number of Gentiles has come in. And so all Israel will be saved, as it is written:

"The deliverer will come from Zion;
he will turn godlessness away from Jacob.
And this is my covenant with them
when I take away their sins" (Romans 11:25-27).

I heard the number of those who were sealed: 144,000 from all the tribes of Israel (Revelation 7:4).

17. *Battle of Armageddon*

They gathered the kings together to the place that in Hebrew is called Armageddon (Revelation 16:16).

See, the LORD is going to lay waste the earth and devastate it. . . . Therefore earth's inhabitants are burned up, and very few are left (Isaiah 24:1,6).

The LORD is angry with all nations; his wrath is upon all their armies. He will totally destroy them. . . . the mountains will be soaked with their blood (Isaiah 34:2-3).

The LORD will strike all the nations that fought against Jerusalem. Their flesh will rot while they are still standing on their feet, their eyes will rot in their sockets, and their tongues will rot in their mouths. On that day men will be stricken by the LORD with great panic (Zechariah 14:12-13).

The beast was captured, and with him the false prophet. . . . The two of them were thrown alive into the fiery lake of burning sulfur (Revelation 19:20).

18. *Fall of Babylon*

> Fallen! Fallen is Babylon the Great!
> She has become a home for demons
> and a haunt for every evil spirit. . . .

> Give her as much torture and grief
> as the glory and luxury she gave herself. . . .
> Therefore in one day her plagues will overtake her:
> death, mourning and famine.
> She will be consumed by fire,
> for mighty is the LORD God who judges her.
> When the Kings of the earth . . . see the smoke of her burning, they will weep and mourn over her. . . .
> Woe! Woe! O great city,
> O Babylon, city of power!
> In one hour your doom has come! (Revelation 18:2, 7-10).

With such violence the great city of Babylon will be thrown down, never to be found again (Revelation 18:21).

19. *Judgment Seat of Christ*

We will all stand before God's judgment seat. . . . So then, each of us will give an account of himself to God (Romans 14:10,12).

We must all appear before the judgment seat of Christ, that each one may receive what is due him for the things done while in the body, whether good or bad (2 Corinthians 5:10).

His work will be shown for what it is. . . . It will be revealed with fire, and the fire will test the quality of each man's work. . . . If it is burned up, he will suffer loss; he himself will be saved, but only as one escaping through the flames (1 Corinthians 3:13-15).

I have fought the good fight, I have finished the race, I have kept the faith. Now there is in store for me the crown of righteousness, which the Lord, the righteous Judge, will award to me on that day—and not only to me, but also to all who have longed for his appearing (2 Timothy 4:7-8).

20. *Triumphal Return of Christ and His Church*

There will be signs in the sun, moon and stars . . . . heavenly bodies will be shaken. At that time they will see the Son of Man coming in a cloud with power and great glory. When these things begin to take place, stand up and lift up your heads, because your redemption is drawing near (Luke 21:25-28).

At that time the sign of the Son of Man will appear in the sky, and all the nations of the earth will mourn. They will see the Son of Man coming on the clouds of the sky, with power and great glory (Matthew 24:30).

The LORD will go out and fight against the nations. . . . On that day his feet will stand on the Mount of Olives, east of Jerusalem, and the Mount of Olives will be split in two from east to west (Zechariah 14:3-4).

> Who is this coming from Edom,
> from Bozrah, with his garments stained crimson?
> Who is this, robed in splendor,
> striding forward in the greatness of his strength? . . .
> I trampled them in my anger
> and trod them down in my wrath;
> their blood splattered my garments,
> and I stained all my clothing.
> For the day of vengeance was in my heart,
> and the year of my redemption has come (Isaiah
> 63:1,3-4).

Multitudes, multitudes
in the valley of decision!
For the day of the LORD is near
in the valley of decision.
The sun and moon will be darkened,
and the stars no longer shine.
The LORD will roar from Zion
and thunder from Jerusalem
the earth and the sky will tremble.
But the LORD will be a refuge for his people,
a stronghold for the people of Israel (Joel 3:14-16).

I saw heaven standing open and there before me was a white horse, whose rider is called Faithful and True. With justice he judges and makes war. His eyes are like blazing fire, and on his head are many crowns. He has a name written on him that no one knows but he himself. He is dressed in a robe dipped in blood, and his name is the Word of God. The armies of heaven were following him, riding on white horses and dressed in fine linen, white and clean. Out of his mouth comes a sharp sword with which to strike down the nations. He will rule them with an iron scepter. He treads the winepress of the fury of the wrath of God Almighty. On his robe and on his thigh he has this name written: KING OF KINGS AND LORD OF LORDS (Revelation 19:11-16).

21. *Judgment of the Nations*

In those days and at that time,
when I restore the fortunes of Judah and Jerusalem,
I will gather all nations
and bring them down to the Valley of Jehoshaphat.
There I will enter into judgment against them
concerning my inheritance, my people Israel (Joel 3:1-2).

When the Son of Man comes in his glory, and all the angels with him, he will sit on his throne in heavenly glory. All the nations will be gathered before him, and he will separate the people one from another as a shepherd separates the sheep from the goats. He will put the sheep on his right and the goats on his left. Then the King will say to those on his right, "Come, you who are blessed by my Father; take your inheritance, the kingdom prepared for you since the creation of the world. . . . " Then he will say to those on his left, "Depart from me, you who are cursed, into the eternal fire prepared for the devil and his angels" (Matthew 25:31-34,41).

22. *Millennial Kingdom*

The beast was captured, and with him the false prophet. . . . The two of them were thrown alive into the fiery lake of burning sulfur. . . . And I saw an angel coming down out of heaven, having the key to the Abyss and holding in his hand a great chain. He seized the dragon, that ancient serpent, who is the devil, or Satan, and bound him for a thousand years. . . . into the abyss (Revelation 19:20–20:3).

You have made them to be a kingdom and priests to serve our God and they will reign on the earth (Revelation 5:10).

They came to life and reigned with Christ a thousand years. . . . This is the first resurrection. . . . The second death has no power over them, but they will be priests of God and of Christ and will reign with him for a thousand years (Revelation 20:4-6).

In the last days the mountain of the LORD's temple will be established as chief among the mountains; it will be raised above the hills and all nations will stream to it. Many peoples will come and say, "Come, let us go up to the mountain of the LORD, to the house of the God of Jacob." . . . The law will go out from Zion, the word of the LORD from

Jerusalem. . . . They will beat their swords into plowshares and their spears into pruning hooks. Nation will not take up sword against nation, nor will they train for war anymore (Isaiah 2:2-4).

> For to us a child is born,
>> to us a son is given,
>> and the government will be on his shoulders.
> And he will be called
>> Wonderful Counselor, Mighty God,
>> Everlasting Father, Prince of Peace.
> Of the increase of his government and peace
>> there will be no end.
> He will reign on David's throne
>> and over his kingdom,
> establishing and upholding it
>> with justice and righteousness
>> from that time on and forever (Isaiah 9:6-7).

23. *Great White Throne Judgment*

When the thousand years are over, Satan will be released from his prison and will go out to deceive the nations . . . to gather them for battle. . . . But fire came down from heaven and devoured them. And the devil, who deceived them, was thrown into the lake of burning sulfur, where the beast and the false prophet had been thrown. They will be tormented day and night for ever and ever.

Then I saw a great white throne and him who was seated on it. Earth and sky fled from his presence, and there was no place for them. And I saw the dead, great and small, standing before the throne, and books were opened. Another book was opened, which is the book of life. . . . death and Hades gave up the dead that were in them, and each person was judged according to what he had done. Then death and Hades were thrown into the lake of fire. The lake of fire is the second death. If anyone's name was not found written in the book of life, he was thrown into the lake of fire (Revelation 20:7-15).

24. *New Heavens and New Earth*

> Behold, I will create
>> new heavens and a new earth.
> The former things will not be remembered,
>> nor will they come to mind. . . .
> I will rejoice over Jerusalem
>> and take delight in my people;
> the sound of weeping and of crying
>> will be heard in it no more. . . .

This is what the LORD says:
> "Heaven is my throne,
>> and earth is my footstool.
> Where is the house you will build for me?
>> Where will my resting place be?
> Has not my hand made all these things,
>> And so they came into being?"(Isaiah 65:17,19;
>> 66:1-2).

I saw a new heaven and a new earth, for the first heaven and the first earth had passed away, and there was no longer any sea. I saw the Holy City, the new Jerusalem, coming down out of heaven from God, prepared as a bride. . . . One of the seven angels . . . said to me, "Come, I will show you the bride, the wife of the Lamb . . . . and he . . . showed me the Holy City, Jerusalem, coming down out of heaven from God. It shone with the glory of God. . . . I did not see a temple in the city, because the Lord God Almighty and the Lamb are its temple. The city does not need the sun or the moon to shine on it, for the glory of God gives it light, and Lamb is its lamp (Revelation 21:1-2,9-11,22-23).

25. *Eternal State*

Multitudes who sleep in the dust of the earth will awake: some to everlasting life, others to shame and everlasting contempt. Those who are wise will shine like the brightness of the heavens, and those who lead many to righteousness, like the stars for ever and ever (Daniel 12:2-3).

Your dead will live;
their bodies will rise.
You who dwell in the dust,
wake up and shout for joy (Isaiah 26:19).

Jesus said to her, "I am the resurrection and the life. He who believes in me will live, even though he dies; and whoever lives and believes in me will never die" (John 11:25-26).

Then the end will come, when he hands over the kingdom to God the Father after he has destroyed all dominion, authority and power. For he must reign until he has put all his enemies under his feet. The last enemy to be destroyed is death. . . . When the perishable has been clothed with imperishable, and the mortal with immortality, then the saying that is written will come true: "Death has been swallowed up in victory" (1 Corinthians 15:24-26,54).

I heard a loud voice from the throne saying, "Now the dwelling of God is with men, and he will live with them. They will be his people, and God himself will be with them and be their God. He will wipe every tear from their eyes. There will be no more death or mourning or crying or pain, for the old order of things has passed away" (Revelation 21:3-4).

The angel showed me the river of the water of life, as clear as crystal, flowing from the throne of God and of the Lamb. . . . On each side of the river stood the tree of life. . . . The throne of God and of the Lamb will be in the city, and his servants will serve him. They will see his face, and his name will be on their foreheads. . . . And they will reign for ever and ever (Revelation 22:1-5).

Whoever believes in the Son has eternal life, but whoever rejects the Son will not see life, for God's wrath remains on him (John 3:36).

Everyone who calls on the name of the Lord will be saved (Romans 10:13).

ABOUT
THE AUTHOR

Dr. Ed Hindson is the Minister of Biblical Studies at the 9,000 member Rehoboth Baptist Church in Atlanta, Georgia, and Vice President of *There's Hope!* He is also distinguished adjunct professor of religion at Liberty University in Lynchburg, Virginia.

Dr. Hindson has authored several books, including: *Angels of Deceit, End Times & the New World Order, No Greater Savior* and *Men of Promise.* He also served as general editor of the *King James Study Bible* and the *Parallel Bible Commentary* and he was one of the translators for the *New King James Version.*

Ed is an executive board member of the Pre-Trib Research Center in Washington, D.C. and he is a Life Fellow of the International Biographical Association of Cambridge, England. Dr. Hindson holds degrees from several institutions: B.A., William Tyndale College; M.A., Trinity Evangelical Divinity School; Th.M., Grace Theological Seminary; Th.D., Trinity College; D.Min., Westminster Theological Seminary; D.Phil., University of South Africa. He has also done graduate study at Acadia University in Nova Scotia, Canada.

Dr. Hindson has served as a visiting lecturer at both Oxford University and the Harvard Divinity School, as well as numerous evangelical seminaries including: Dallas, Denver, Trinity, Grace and Westminster. Hindson combines solid academic scholarship with a dynamic and practical teaching style that communicates biblical truth in a powerful and posititve manner.

ENDNOTES

Chapter 1: Understanding the End Times

1. Quotation from the Christic Institute in E. Dobson and E. Hindson, "Apocalypse Now? What Fundamentalists Believe About the End of the World," in *Policy Review* (Fall 1986), pp. 16-22.
2. For a detailed study, see Herman Hoyt, *The End Times* (Chicago: Moody, 1969), pp. 9-10, 63-65.
3. See the excellent discussions of J.D. Pentecost, *Things to Come* (Grand Rapids: Zondervan, 1964), pp. 239-50; and Alva McClain, *Daniel's Prophecy of the Seventy Weeks* (Grand Rapids: Zondervan, 1940).
4. Robert Anderson, *The Coming Prince* (London: Hodder & Stoughten, 1909).
5. Cf. Elias Bickerman, *From Ezra to the Last of the Maccabees* (New York: Schoken, 1966); D.S. Russell, *Between the Testaments* (London: SCM Press, 1960); John Rogerson, *Atlas of the Bible* (New York: Facts on File, 1985), pp. 36-39.
6. *See* "Temple, Herod's" in *Eerdmans' Bible Dictionary* (Grand Rapids: Eerdmans, 1987), pp. 991-92; T. Cornell and J. Matthews, *Atlas of the Roman World* (New York: Facts on File, 1982), pp. 79-81, 162-64.
7. *See* "Diaspora of the Jews," in W.A. Elwell, ed., *Baker Encyclopedia of the Bible* (Grand Rapids: Baker, 1988), vol. 1, pp. 623-25; Nicolas de Lange, *Atlas of the Jewish World* (New York: Facts on File, 1984), pp. 46-53.
8. *See* Revelation 5:6-14; 14:1-5; 19:19; 21:9, 22-23; 22:1-3.

Chapter 2: Separating Fact from Fiction in Bible Prophecy

1. Edgar C. Whisenant, *88 Reasons Why the Rapture Will Be in 1988* (Nashville: World Bible Society, 1988).
2. Harold Camping, *1994?* (New York: Vantage Press, 1992). Contra, cf. B.J. Oropeza, *99 Reasons Why No One Knows When Christ Will Return* (Downers Grove, IL: InterVarsity Press, 1994) and David Reagan, *The Master Plan* (Eugene, OR: Harvest House, 1993).
3. Cf. *Babylonian Talmud*, vol. 1; Martin Luther, Supputatio Annorum Mundi (1541); Phillip Melanchthon, *Carion's Chronicle* (1550), Introduction, Folio Vi. For details see Edward E. Hindson, *The Puritans' Use of Scripture in the Development of an Apocalyptical Hermeneutic* (Pretoria: University of South Africa, 1984), pp. 17-31.

4. Daniel R. Mitchell, *"Is the Rapture on Schedule?"* National Liberty Journal (October 1988), p. 66.

5. One of the worst examples of excessive prophetic speculation is J.R. Church, *Hidden Prophecies in the Psalms* (Oklahoma City, OK: Prophecy Publications, 1986). He finds British General Allenby in Psalm 17 conquering Jerusalem in 1917; Psalm 39-44 telling the story of the Holocaust from 1939 to 1944; and Psalm 48 predicting the birth of Israel in 1948.

6. Cf. Ed Dobson and Ed Hindson, "Armageddon Theology: Preaching Politics and the End of the World," in *The Seduction of Power* (Old Tappan, NJ: Revell, 1988),pp. 77-92. Also, Ed Dobson and Ed Hindson, "Apocalypse Now? What Fundamentalists Believe About the End of the World," *Policy Review* (Fall 1986), pp. 16-22.

7. See Lorraine Boettner, *The Millennium* (Philadelphia: Presbyterian & Reformed, 1957); J.M. Kik, *An Eschatology of Victory* (Philadelphia: Presbyterian & Reformed, 1971); R.J. Rushdoony, *Thy Kingdom Come* (Fairfax, VA: Chalcedon, 1975); David Chilton, Paradise Restored (Tyler, TX: Dominion, 1984); J.J. Davis, *Christ's Victorious Kingdom* (Grand Rapids: Baker, 1986).

8. See J.E. Adams, *The Time Is at Hand* (Philadelphia: Presbyterian & Reformed, 1970); G.C. Berkouwer, *The Return of Christ* (Grand Rapids: Eerdmans, 1962); P.E. Hughes, *Interpreting Prophecy* (Grand Rapids: Eerdmans, 1976); and A. Hoekema, *The Bible and the Future* (Grand Rapids: Eerdmans, 1979).

9. See H.A. Hoyt, *The End Times* (Chicago: Moody, 1969); Rene Pache, *The Return of Jesus Christ* (Chicago: Moody Press, 1955); J.D. Pentecost, *Things to Come* (Grand Rapids: Zondervan, 1958); Tim LaHaye, *The Beginning of the End* (Wheaton, IL: Tyndale House, 1972); Leon Wood, *The Bible and Future Events* (Grand Rapids: Zondervan, 1973); John Walvoord, *Major Bible Prophecies* (New York: Harper Collins, 1991).

10. Cf. Allen Beechick, *The Pre-Tribulation Rapture* (Denver: Accent, 1980); Guy Duty, *Escape from the Coming Tribulation* (Minneapolis: Bethany Fellowship, 1975); J. Walvoord, *The Blessed Hope and the Tribulation* (Grand Rapids: Zondervan, 1975); G.E. Ladd, *The Blessed Hope* (Grand Rapids: Eerdmans, 1956); R.H. Gundry, *The Church and the Tribulation* (Grand Rapids: Zondervan, 1973); H. Lindsell, *The Gathering Storm* (Wheaton, IL: Tyndale House, 1980); M.J. Erickson, *Contemporary Options in Eschatology* (Grand Rapids: Baker, 1977).

11. David Jeremiah, *Escape the Coming Night* (Dallas: Word, 1990), p. 85.

12. See Dobson and Hindson, *The Seduction of Power*, p. 90ff. for details.

13. Frank Peretti, *This Present Darkness* (Westchester, IL: Crossway, 1986), emphasizes this in a graphic form in his bestselling novel.

Chapter 3: Signs of the End Times

1. John Walvoord, *Matthew: Thy Kingdom Come* (Chicago: Moody, 1974), p. 181. Cf. also E. Hindson, "Matthew," in *Liberty Study Bible*, ed. E. Hindson and W. Kroll (Nashville: Thomas Nelson, 1983), pp. 1946-52.
2. Cf. Homer Kent, Jr., "Matthew," in *Wycliffe Bible Commentary* (Chicago: Moody, 1962), p. 85ff.
3. William S. LaSor, *The Truth About Armageddon* (Grand Rapids: Baker, 1982), p. 15.
4. J.P. Lange, *Commentary on the Holy Scriptures: Matthew* (Grand Rapids: Zondervan, n.d.), p. 428.
5. W.F. Arndt and F.W. Gingrich, *A Greek-English Lexicon of the New Testament* (Chicago:University of Chicago, 1957), p. 153.
6. Kent, "Matthew," p. 89.
7. LaSor, *The Truth About Armageddon*, p. 122.
8. See Amos 5:18-20; Joel 1:15; 2:1,11,31; Isaiah 2:11-19; 13:6-9; 22:5; 34:8; Jeremiah 46:10; Zephaniah 1:7-8; Ezekiel 7:10; 13:5; 30:3; and Zechariah 14:1.
9. Charles Dyer, *The Rise of Babylon* (Wheaton, IL: Tyndale House, 1991) makes a great deal out of Hussein's attempt to refurnish the excavated ruins of ancient Babylon as if this were a fulfillment of prophecy. Yet the *Washington Post* (10 Feb. 1975, sec. A, p. 5) reported that an Italian archaeologist had been employed by the pre-Hussein government of Iraq to rebuild the Tower of Babel over 15 years ago.

Chapter 4: What's Next on the Prophetic Calendar?

1. These thoughts are developed from E. Dobson and E. Hindson, *The Seduction of Power* (Old Tappan, NJ: Revell, 1988), pp. 93-109.
2. Paul Johnson, *Modern Times: The World from the Twenties to the Eighties* (San Francisco: Harper & Row, 1983).
3. Charles Colson, *Against the Night* (Ann Arbor, MI: Servant, 1989), p. 19.
4. For an excellent assessment of these ideas, cf. Donald Bloesch, *Crumbling Foundations* (Grand Rapids: Zondervan, 1984); Harvey Cox, *Religion in the Secular City* (New York: Simon & Schuster, 1984); Carl F.H. Henry, *The Christian Mindset in a Secular Society* (Portland: Multnomah Press, 1984); Tim LaHaye, *The Race for the 21st Century* (Nashville: Thomas Nelson, 1986); Richard Neuhaus, *The Naked Public Square* (Grand Rapids: Eerdmans, 1984); R.C. Sproul, *Lifeviews: Understanding the Ideas That Shape Society* (Old Tappan, NJ: Revell, 1986); and Cal Thomas, *The Death of Ethics in America* (Waco, TX: Word, 1988).

5. Allan Bloom, *The Closing of the American Mind* (New York: Simon & Schuster, 1987). The author argues that higher education has been hijacked by a system of philosophy that has impoverished the souls of today's students.

6. Ibid., p. 34.

7. Arthur Levine, *When Dreams and Heroes Died: A Portrait of Today's College Student* (San Francisco: Jossey-Bass, 1980). Levine's study, sponsored by the Carnegie Foundation for the Advancement of Teaching, found that today's students are self-centered "escapists" who want little responsibility for solving society's problems.

8. See Karen Hoyt, *The New Age Rage* (Old Tappan, NJ: Revell, 1987) and Elliot Miller, *A Crash Course on the New Age Movement* (Grand Rapids: Baker, 1989).

9. Francis Schaeffer, *Escape from Reason* (Chicago: InterVarsity, 1965).

10. Rene Pache, *The Return of Jesus Christ* (Chicago: Moody, 1955) p. 109.

11. See Allen Beechick, *The Pre-Tribulation Rapture* (Denver: Accent, 1980); Guy Duty, *Escape from the Coming Tribulation* (Minneapolis: Bethany Fellowship, 1975); John Walvoord, *The Blessed Hope and the Tribulation* (Grand Rapids: Zondervan, 1975).

12. *See* J.O. Buswell, *A Systematic Theology of the Christian Religion* (Grand Rapids: Zondervan, 1962), vol. 2, pp. 393-450; N.B. Harrison, *The End* (Minneapolis: Harrison, 1941); M. Rosenthal, *The Pre-Wrath Rapture* (Nashville: Thomas Nelson, 1990).

13. See G.E. Ladd, *The Blessed Hope* (Grand Rapids: Eerdmans, 1956); R.H. Gundry, *The Church and the Tribulation* (Grand Rapids: Zondervan, 1973).

Chapter 5: The Coming Darkness

1. Quoted by Charles Colson, *Against the Night* (Ann Arbor, MI: Servant, 1989), p. 55.

2. Ibid., pp. 133-34.

3. 2 Thessalonians 2:3.

4. Peter Lalonde, *One World Under Antichrist* (Eugene, OR: Harvest House, 1991), p. 58.

5. Barbara Marx Hubbard, *The Book of Co-Creation: An Evolutionary Interpretation of the New Testament.* Unpublished manuscript, dated 1980. Quoted by Lalonde, pp. 166-67.

6. Lalonde, p. 173.

7. Michael Horton, ed. *The Agony of Deceit* (Chicago: Moody Press, 1990).

8. Marvin Stone, "What Kind of People Are We?" *U.S. News & World Report,* February 5, 1979.

Chapter 6: The Gathering Storm

1. Commonly reported in the new media on Feb. 8, 1991.
2. Quoted by John Phillips, *Only God Can Prophesy!* (Wheaton, IL: Harold Shaw, 1975), p. 27.
3. Arthur Levine, *When Dreams and Heroes Died: A Portrait of Today's College Student* (San Francisco: Jossey-Bass, 1980). Cf. also Alan Bloom, *The Closing of the American Mind* (New York: Simon & Schuster, 1986).
4. See Phillips, *Only God Can Prophesy!* pp. 105-07.
5. Ibid., pp. 111-12.
6. "A War Against the Earth," *Time*, Feb. 4, 1991, pp. 32-33.
7. Dave Hunt, *Global Peace and the Rise of the Antichrist* (Eugene, OR: Harvest House, 1990), p. 163.
8. "Playing with Fire," *Time*, 18 Sept. 1989, pp. 76-80.
9. "Europe Starts Federation Process," *St. Louis Post-Dispatch*, 12 Nov. 1990, A3.
10. *Europe*, Nov. 1989, p. 20ff.
11. Steve Ludwig, "Electronic Money Will Change Your Life," *Sky* Jan. 1974, pp. 1921.
12. Robert Reich, *The Work of Nations* (New York: Alfred Knopf, 1991), p. 8.
13. Ibid., p. 63.
14. Ibid., p. 77.
15. Pat Robertson, *The New World Order* (Dallas: Word Books, 1991), p. 191.
16. Chuck Colson and Jack Eckerd, *Why America Doesn't Work* (Dallas: Word Books, 1991), pp. 179-80.
17. Ibid.
18. Jack Kemp, "How We Trap America's Poor in the 'Other Economy,'" *Washington Post* May 26, 1991, D1.
19. Cf. Robertson, *The New World Order*, p. 35.
20. Elliot Miller, *A Crash Course on the New Age Movement* (Grand Rapids: Baker, 1989), p. 15.
21. Ibid., p. 18.
22. Ibid., p. 116.
23. Constance Cumbey, *The Hidden Dangers of the Rainbow* (Lafayette, LA: Huntington House, 1983).
24. John MacArthur, Jr., *God, Satan and Angels* (Panorama City, CA: Word of Grace, 1983), p. 68.
25. Ralph P. Martin, *Broadman Bible Commentary* (Nashville: Broadman Press, 1971), p. 174. Cf. Romans 8:38; Ephesians 1:21; 3:10.

Chapter 7: The Struggle for World Dominion

1. Malachi Martin, *The Keys of This Blood: The Struggle for World Dominion Between Pope John Paul II, Mikhail Gorbachev, & the Capitalist West* (New York: Simon & Schuster, 1990).

2. Charles Colson, *Against the Night* (Ann Arbor, MI: Servant Publications, 1989), p. 19.
3. Robert Hughes, "The Fraying of America," *Time*, Feb. 3, 1992, p. 44.
4. Quoted by Hughes, ibid.
5. Peter Lalonde, *One World Under Antichrist* (Eugene, OR: Harvest House, 1991), pp. 20-24.
6. Ibid., p. 23.
7. George Bush, "Address to the Nation," September 16, 1990.
8. *Time*, Dec. 11, 1989, front cover.
9. Ibid., p. 34.
10. Martin, *The Keys of This Blood*, p. 18.
11. Ibid., p. 117.
12. Henrik Bering-Jensen, "Germany Resurgent," *Insight on the News*, Mar. 23, 1992, p. 7.
13. Ibid., p. 8.
14. Reported in the press, June 8, 1990.

Chapter 8: Can There Be Peace in the Middle East?

1. "Don't Get Left in the Dust," *Newsweek*, Sept. 27, 1993, pp. 20-29. Cf. also "History in a Handshake," *Time*, Sept. 27, 1993.
2. Henry Kissinger, "Turning a Fairy Tale into Reality," *Newsweek*, Sept. 27, 1993, pp. 32-33. Cf. also "Peace at Last?" *Newsweek*, Sept. 13, 1993, cover story.
3. This position is advocated by John Walvoord in *Armageddon, Oil and the Middle East Crisis* (Grand Rapids: Zondervan, 1990), pp. 129-35.
4. Ibid., p. 131.
5. See John Lamb, "Power to the People," in *1992 Now*, published by IBM Europe, Mar. 1989, pp. 8-9; and "Reshaping Europe: 1992 and Beyond," *Business Week*, Dec. 12, 1988, pp. 48-51.
6. See Dave Hunt, *Global Peace and the Rise of the Antichrist* (Eugene, OR: Harvest House, 1990); David Reagan, *The Master Plan* (Eugene, OR: Harvest House, 1993). This position was argued earlier by Tim LaHaye, *The Coming Peace in the Middle East* (Grand Rapids: Zondervan, 1984).
7. Nicholas de Lange, *Atlas of the Jewish World* (New York: Facts on File, 1984), pp. 38-41. He cites large Jewish populations at Baghdad, Cairo, Ghazna, and Samarkand during the Middle Ages.
8. Abba Eban, *My People: The Story of the Jews* (New York: Random House, 1968), p. 51.
9. John Phillips, *Only God Can Prophesy!* (Wheaton, IL: Harold Shaw, 1975), p. 61.
10. John Walvoord, *Armageddon, Oil and the Middle East Crisis*, pp. 49-51.
11. Ibid., p. 129.

Chapter 9: Rips in the Islamic Curtain

1. Dave Hunt, *Global Peace and the Rise of the Antichrist* (Eugene, OR: Harvest House), p. 220.
2. Ibid., p. 223.
3. Hal Lindsey is the author of the best-selling book *Late Great Planet Earth* (Grand Rapids: Zondervan, 1970), and a popular prophecy teacher.
4. Dave Hunt, *Global Peace and the Rise of the Antichrist*, p. 5.
5. *Time*, Jan. 28, 1991, p. 70.
6. John Walvoord, *Armageddon, Oil and the Middle East Crisis* (Grand Rapids: Zondervan, 1990), p. 18.
7. Benjamin Barber, "Jihad vs. McWorld," *The Atlantic*, March 1992, pp. 53-63.
8. Ibid., p. 53.
9. The identification of these names has been verified by extensive archaeological research and is to be preferred over identifications often given in popular books on prophecy. For a detailed examination of the evidence, see E.M. Yamauchi, *Foes from the Northern Frontier* (Grand Rapids: Baker, 1982), and E.D. Phillips, "The Scythian Domination in Western Asia: Its Record in History, Scripture and Archaeology," *World Archaeology*, 1972, p. 129ff.
10. Walvoord, *Armageddon, Oil and the Middle East Crisis*, pp. 137-47.
11. Yamauchi, *Foes from the Northern Frontier*, pp. 29-36, 63-68.
12. Charles Dyer, *The Rise of Babylon* (Wheaton, IL: Tyndale House, 1991), pp. 161-204.
13. Gleason Archer, "Isaiah," *Wycliffe Bible Commentary* (Chicago: Moody, 1962), p. 621. Cf. also E. Hindson, "Isaiah," *Liberty Bible Commentary* (Nashville: Thomas Nelson, 1983), p. 1322ff.
14. For an excellent history of ancient Babylon, see Joan Oates, *Babylon* (London: Thomas & Hudson, 1979); H.W.F. Saggs, *The Greatness That Was Babylon* (New York: Macmillan, 1962); and E.M. Yamauchi, "Babylon," in R.K. Harrison, ed., *Major Cities of the Biblical World* (Nashville: Thomas Nelson, 1985), pp. 32-48.
15. Oates, *Babylon*, pp. 139-43.
16. Ibid., p. 143.
17. Dyer, *The Rise of Babylon*, p. 192.
18. Ibid., p. 190.
19. Isaiah delivered oracles against Babylon (13:1), Assyria (14:25), Philistia (14:29), Moab (15:1), Damascus (17:1), Cush (18:1), Egypt (19:1), the Desert (21:1), Edom (21:11), Arabia (21:13), and Tyre (23:1).
20. W.A. VanGemeren, "Isaiah," in W. Elwell, ed., *Evangelical Commentary on the Bible* (Grand Rapids: Baker, 1989), p. 484.

Chapter 10: Globalism The New World Order

1. John Naisbitt and Patricia Aburdene, *Megatrends 2000* (New York: William Morrow, 1990).
2. Dave Hunt, *Global Peace and the Rise of the Antichrist* (Eugene, OR: Harvest House, 1990), p. 55.
3. *Time*, Dec.11, 1989, p. 37.
4. Hunt, *Global Peace*, pp. 60-61.
5. *Time*, Jan. 7, 1991, p. 23.
6. Commonly televised Jan. 16, 1991, and reported in the press, Jan. 17, 1991.
7. "Turning Visions into Reality," *Time*, Dec.11, 1989, p. 36.
8. Dave Hunt, *The Coming Peace* (Eugene, OR: Harvest House, 1990).
9. "Gorbachev, God and Socialism," *Time*, Dec.11, 1989, p. 38.
10. See the insightful comments of David Jeremiah, *Escape the Coming Night* (Dallas: Word, 1990), pp. 167-81. He notes that the great prostitute of the end times has two faces: apostasy and religion.
11. George Will, "Europe's Second Reformation," *Newsweek*, Nov. 20, 1989, p. 90.
12. "Charging Ahead," *Time*, Sept. 18, 1989, pp. 40-45.
13. Ibid., p. 43.
14. *U.S. News & World Report*, Oct.15, 1990, p. 64.
15. Naisbitt and Aburdene, *Megatrends 2000*, pp. 49-50.
16. Eric Salama, "Europe's New Shop Window," in *1992 Now*, published by IBM Europe, March 1989, p. 5.
17. Nicholas Colchester, "Freeing the Frontiers," *1992 Now*, p. 6.
18. John Lamb, "Power to the People," *1992 Now*, pp. 8-9.
19. Ibid., p. 9.
20. Hunt, *Global Peace*, p. 73.

Chapter 11: What's Ahead for the 21st Century?

1. John Naisbitt and Patricia Aburdene, *Megatrends 2000* (New York: William Morrow, 1990), p. 11.
2. Russell Chandler, *Racing Toward 2001* (San Francisco: HarperCollins, 1992), pp. 45-47.
3. Ibid., p. 46.
4. Ibid., p. 47.
5. Ibid., p. 46.
6. Neil Postman, *Amusing Ourselves to Death* (New York: Penguin Books, 1986), p. 6.
7. Ernst Cassirer, *An Essay on Man* (Garden City, NY: Doubleday, 1956), p. 43. Quoted by Postman, p. 10.
8. Ed Dobson and Ed Hindson, *The Seduction of Power* (Old Tappan, NJ: Revell, 1988), p. 93.

9. Allan Bloom, *The Closing of the American Mind* (New York: Simon & Schuster, 1987), p. 85.
10. Francis Schaeffer, *The Great Evangelical Disaster* (Westchester, IL: Crossway Books, 1984), pp. 141-51.
11. Francis Schaeffer and C. Everett Koop, *Whatever Happened to the Human Race?* (Old Tappan, NJ: Revell, 1979).
12. R.C. Sproul, *Lifeviews: Understanding the Ideas That Shape Society Today* (Old Tappan, NJ: Revell, 1986), p. 62.
13. John MacArthur, Jr., *Our Sufficiency in Christ* (Dallas: Word, 1991), p. 19.
14. Naisbitt and Aburdene, *Megatrends 2000*, p. 304.
15. Elmer Towns, *Ten of Today's Most Innovative Churches* (Ventura, CA: Regal Books, 1991).
16. George Barna, *Successful Churches: What They Have in Common* (Glendale, CA: Barna Research Group, 1990).
17. Chandler, *Racing Toward 2001*, p. 92.
18. Ibid., p. 96.
19. J. Conway, *Adult Children of Divorce* (Downers Grove, IL: InterVarsity Press, 1990).
20. Quoted in *Progressions*, A Lilly Endowment Occasional Report 2, no. 1, 1990, p. 20.
21. *Religious News Service* Nov. 1988, p.15.
22. James D. Hunter, *Evangelicalism: The Coming Generation* (Chicago: University of Chicago Press, 1987).

Chapter 12: Where Do We Go from Here?

1. Dave Hunt, *Global Peace and the Rise of Antichrist* (Eugene, OR: Harvest House, 1990), p. 280.
2. Ibid., p. 283.

Chapter 13: It Isn't Over till It's Over

1. The interpretation of Isaiah's "Little Apocalypse" (Isaiah 24) hinges on the translation of the Hebrew word *erats*. The KJV translates it "earth" six times and "land" three times, whereas the RSV and NIV translate it "earth" each time. The interpretation revolves around whether the judgments described here refer to the whole earth or just the land of Israel. In verse 4, *erets* is used in parallel with *tebel*, the Hebrew word for "world." Edward Young, *The Book of Isaiah* (Grand Rapids: Eerdmans, 1965), vol. 2, p. 154, quotes Kittel in asserting that *tebel* is never restricted to the land of Judah. There can be no doubt, then, that Isaiah has the whole world in view in this prophecy.
2. See E. Hindson, "Isaiah," in E. Hindson and W. Kroll, eds., *Liberty Bible Commentary* (Nashville: Thomas Nelson, 1983), pp. 1335-38, 1350-51; and Gleason Archer, "Isaiah," *Wycliffe Bible Commentary* (Chicago: Moody, 1962), p. 633.